HOW TO BUY AN ELEPHANT

And 38 Other Things You Never Knew

You Wanted to Know!

HOW TO
BUY AN ELEPHANT

And 38 Other Things You Never Knew You Wanted to Know!

JOHN KRAUSZ

SKYHORSE PUBLISHING

> **WARNING:**
> Some of the activities described in this book are
> DANGEROUS. Many of the processes, procedures, and techniques
> are OUTDATED and INVALID. The publisher cannot accept any
> responsibility for harm that results from readers following any of the
> information or advice provided in this book.

www.skyhorsepublishing.com

Book design by Mark McGarry
Set in Garamond

Library of Congress Cataloging-in-Publication Data
Krausz, John.
How to buy an elephant : and 38 other things you
never knew you wanted to know / by John Krausz.
p. cm.
Originally published: New York : Hawthorn Books, c1977.
ISBN-13: 978-1-60239-106-2 (alk. paper)
ISBN-10: 1-60239-106-8 (alk. paper)
1. Curiosities and wonders.
2. Handbooks, vade-mecums, etc. I. Title.

AG243.K76 2007   031.02-dc22
2007015367

10 9 8 7 6 5 4 3 2 1

Printed in China

Contents

INTRODUCTION

❧ ❦

AT FIRST, the title "How to Buy an Elephant" was just a wise-guy conceit, a reference to the old-style elephant jokes, which ran something like this:

First Man: Have I got a deal for you, an elephant for only $500!

Second Man: I haven't the room, and what would I want with an elephant?

First Man: Okay, how about two for five hundred?

Second Man: Now you're talking!

Then I was faced with those most literal of people, editors and publishers. They *really* wanted to know. How *do* you buy an elephant? So I'd run a little riff; "Well, the first three rules are:

1. You want an Asian elephant, they're easier to train.

2. You want a female, not a male. Males go into "must,"

which is something like going into heat, and after all, they weigh five thousand pounds.

3. You want a little one, not more than three years old. You wouldn't want it to have bad habits, and it would cost less to ship."

Accidentally I heard a TV panel show talking about "What animal would you choose if you were on a desert island?" and the panel to a man said, "A cow for the milk," which shows a lack of knowledge of bovine biology, but I was still surprised to hear the expert say, "An elephant; they live a long time, learn to do a great many things, and are good company."

My routine was complete; I proceeded to ignore the question. *How to Buy an Elephant* was just what the book was called. It was *about* "things you didn't know you wanted to know," and I had lots of things that I wanted to check out . . . How do you ride a high wheeler? (p. 16) How do you take a shower bath? (p. 167) How do you have good posture? (p. 184) I also had material that I had run out of people to show, like "The Dangers of Tight-Lacing" (p. 68), "The Bedroom Chair as Gymnasium" (p. 206), and "Whom and When to Marry" (p. 25).

I knew that I would find things that I wasn't looking for that I would also want to include. "The Art of Mind-Reading Revealed" (p. 59) and "Weather Prognostics" (p. 195) are some of the things that jumped into view in the process of putting this book together.

I had some Government Printing Office material that I thought others should see, especially "How to Climb a Ladder" (p. 86), since over the years I have known quite a number of people who hurt themselves by not knowing how. And "Signal to Cranes" (p. 52) appeals to the Walter Mitty in each of us.

Some that beg to be read out loud, I have hoarded to myself for many years. I am finally sharing these secret treasures: "Forster

Powell: The Celebrated Pedestrian" (p. 164) and Lieutenant Colonel Baron de Berenger's "If Attacked by a Bull" (p. 23) and "Protecting Life and Property: Safety on the Highways when Traveling" (p. 96).

I've put in some favorite bits of history: information on how to ride a railway train (p. 188), "Pneumatic Railways and Rapid Transit in NYC" (p. 146), and, of course, plenty of material about elephants. A friend with access to a computer produced several pounds of printed pages, and I read through story after story of "unmanageable elephants" that had to be disposed of in one grotesque manner or another, so it seemed logical that the Asian elephant had been placed on the endangered species list, and it was obvious that the African would soon be there also. Then the fact that two of the largest wild animal dealers on the East Coast had recently gone out of business seemed ominous in some way.

The only cheerful note was that the Central Park Zoo's African female, which is on loan to the Knoxville Zoo for breeding, was pregnant [1977]. This will be the first African elephant ever born in America. My *beau-jest* had turned quite bitter. My three rules were more or less true and in their truth had proved damaging to the further existence of elephants: Most imported elephants have been Asian, female, and immature, thus reducing the breeding stock.

The TV expert also proved correct. Elephants do live a long time, learn very difficult things, and, not only that, they make good babysitters, too! (See "The Elephant at Work" [p. 213]).

I have included "Jumbo and the White Elephant War" (p. 5) purely because I thought it was fine reading—one of my principal reasons for choosing anything for this book I wish that there were some way that I could thank the many authors whose work I have used—and probably misused, because the longer articles had to be cut and rearranged and in some cases rewritten. They had more time and room in those days to express themselves, and I hope that I have not done too much violence to their ideas in my handling of them.

I also thank my editor, my family, and my friends for being so forbearing during this difficult time. Any measure of success this book may have is a result of their leaving me strictly alone to brood.

John Krausz

How *Do* You Buy an Elephant?

John Krausz, 1977

❧ ❧

THE BUYING of an elephant is increasingly difficult for anyone, circus, zoo dealer, or eccentric. At present the Asian elephant, male and female, is on the endangered species list, making importation impossible and raising current costs of already imported animals to an unprecedented high. Only Southwick's Bird & Animal Farm in Blackstone, Massachusetts, remains in business as a major East Coast importer of elephants. While owners of elephants will claim that no two have ever been bought in the same way, the majority of animals are in fact purchased through dealers.

Barnum & Bailey Circus has purchased all its elephants either from dealers or small circuses that were going out of business. They would never buy an animal from a zoo, since it would either be badly trained or an unmanageable animal—nor do they bother to buy elephants from foreign dealers or governments, since it's too complicated and time consuming. All of their elephants are bought for performing purposes, and while they have Africans as well as Asians, they claim the Africans are stupider and harder to train. (One man can get an elephant act trained and together in six months.) In the past they have paid dealers approximately $7,500 for Asian elephants—off the boat from India—with permits provided by the dealers and no quarantine necessary.

The Bronx Zoo bought their elephants with the intention of breeding Asians in this country and thereby avoiding the problems of their status as endangered. In the fall of '73 they bought three females and one male—paying $4,600 per elephant—through

Danny Southwick, the late Massachusetts import mogul.

They also have one African female, who, despite African elephants' reputation for being "harder to handle," has not been more difficult than their four Asians. She is currently on loan to the Knoxville Zoo—for mating—and on writing of this article she has just become pregnant (Summer 1977). No African elephant has ever been born in the U.S. until now.

Central Park Zoo has one Asian female that they paid $3,000 for in 1963, bought from Trefflich's, a large N.Y. animal dealing company that has gone out of business. Trefflich's, in turn, had bought this same elephant from Deitch's—a large animal farm in Fairlane, New Jersey, which is also out of business.

As for the dealers themselves, they buy elephants not only from countries of origin—Kenya, Thailand, India, etc.—but also from all of the same sources they sell to. Often a circus going out of business, another dealer, a small animal park, or private zoo will sell an elephant already in the U.S. to a dealer.

Before the Endangered Species Act of Dec. 28, 1973, buying elephants from the foregoing countries required having contacts in those countries, either trapper/dealers or the governments themselves; applying for permits from the U.S. Department of Agriculture (Fish and Wildlife Division); and paying for shipping costs. According to Southwick's, the average age of imported elephants was two years old, and they were generally less than fifty inches high. The majority of orders were for females, and all the animals arrived at JFK airport—one of thirteen approved ports of entry for wild animals. The shipping itself costs approximately $1,500 to $2,000 ($2.60 per pound: the elephant weighs 600 to 800 pounds without its crate). Their traveling accommodations from India included a wooden framed cage; their legs were tied to the frames for the 14- to 15-hour flight. From Kenya they traveled in wooden boxes with metal trays at the bottom (for droppings) and open board tops, fronts, and backs.

Southwick's Asian sources (which are no longer operational, now that permits for importation cannot be obtained) included trapper/dealers in Bangkok, Thai-

land, and the Delhi area of India. Their African source is a dealer in Kenya who owns a small farm, hires trappers, and ships animals all over the world. While the Asians previously imported arrived partially trained—not for tricks but for handling—the Africans are wild upon arrival.

The current prices—1977—are quoted at: Africans, $7,500; Asians (already in this country), $15,000. And delivery—from time of ordering—is usually upwards of two months.

In order to bring an elephant into the U.S., a permit for importa-

tion must be obtained from the Department of Agriculture, Fish and Wildlife Division, and while there is no cost for such permission, certain criteria must be met. These criteria involve inspection of the grounds and facilities provided for the elephant, the handlers' expertise, and availability of veterinary care. It is for this reason that individual parties find it impossible to receive the necessary permission, and importation is restricted to animal farms, dealers, zoos, and circuses.

While the passage of the Endangered Species Act (Dec. 28, 1973) has made it illegal or virtually impossible to import Asian elephants, some consideration is given to whether the animal was purchased before the bill was passed and to whether it was born in captivity or in the wild.

Africans—which do not fall under this act—still require permits and clearance through the Federal Register before being admitted to this country, and the government specifies a period of 90 to 120 days for such permission to clear.

Do Elephants Snore?

Mammal curator at the Bronx Zoo, Mr. MacNamara, said he couldn't tell because their stomachs rumble so loudly when they sleep, you can't hear anything else.

Central Park Zoo reports it's difficult to sneak up on an elephant to find out! They don't like to be caught on their sides and will wake when anyone approaches close enough to find out. But they do make a strange gasping sound . . .

Jumbo & the White Elephant War

W. C. THOMPSON, *ON THE ROAD WITH THE CIRCUS* (1903)

❧ ❧

Jumbo was the biggest elephant ever in this country, and few are in on the secret that the tremendous success of the animal's tour was an accident of fortune," observed our elephant man. "He was an African animal and very stupid, but always good-natured. An agent of the big American circus heard that he was the tallest pachyderm in captivity and that London was anxious to sell him. The man closed the sale for two thousand pounds, with no conception of the money-making prize he was securing. The beast had been a pet with the children in the London Zoological Gardens, but the announcement of his purchase by Americans was received with no especial expressions of regret. It required two weeks to build a van-like cage for the journey by sea, and then keepers went to the zoo to lead Jumbo to the ship. He strode along all right until the gate of the garden closed behind them and then lay down in the street. It was a pure case of elephantine obstinacy, and the animal wouldn't budge. There he measured his length in the dust for twenty-four hours despite all urging and entreaty, to the despair of his custodians, who little realized the wonderful effect the incident would have on the owner's pocketbook.

"The English newspapers soon heard of the occurrence and promptly seized upon it for an effective 'story.' 'Dear old Jumbo,' they said, 'refused to leave the scene of his happy days with the children; his exhibition of protest was one of remarkable sagacity; they hoped he would continue to defy the Yankee showmen and remain in London; he was the pet and friend of the little ones and ought never to have been disposed of, any way.' The elephant when in repose or resistance rests on his knees, and one of the newspapers sagely remarked that Jumbo was in an attitude of prayer. The Humane Society was appealed to and someone made a sympathetic hit by telling how lonesome and melancholy was Alice, the abandoned 'wife.' The pathos of the thing was very affecting, on the surface, but a phenomenal advertisement.

"The animal finally got on his feet and marched to the boat. Weeping women and children lined the way. The circus owners were then alive to the possibilities and, concealing their identity, got out an injunction, 'in the interests of the London public,' attempting to restrain the brute's departure. Of course, it was dissolved, but it kept feeling at high pitch up to the time of sailing. I remember the Baroness Burdett-Coutts and a party of distinguished companions visited the steamer to say good-bye and left a big box of buns, of which Jumbo was very fond, for his use during the voyage.

"The story of the brute's reluctance to leave his young friends in England was broadcast and he became the feature of the circus, whereas otherwise he would probably have attracted only passing attention. It was his own fortuitous conduct and not the superior skill of the showman that made his circus career so profitable. Jumbo was killed by a train at St. Thomas, Ontario, in July, 1885. A dwarf elephant with him escaped injury, and the show made some capital by asserting that the big elephant sacrificed his own life in shielding his small companion. As a matter of fact, he was seized with another fit of unyielding stubbornness and wouldn't step down an embankment out of an express's path. He was never south of Louisville or west of Omaha. Matthew Scott was his keeper. He shared not only his bed, but his bread and tobacco with his charge. After the brute's death he followed the circus wherever it went, and during the winter visited almost daily the preserved skin and bones of his late companion.

"There was, of course, a Jumbo II, but he was nowhere near the size of the original beast. Harnessed with electrodes and other apparatus he stood in the middle of the Stadium at the Exposition Grounds at Buffalo, N.Y., on November 9, 1901, and gave the world a practical demonstration that an elephant can take twenty-two hundred volts of electricity with apparent unconcern. If the electric current reached his nerves he manifested no sign of it. Electric wires had been run from the Exposition power house to what was to be Jumbo II's death platform, and when the signal was given, twenty-two hundred volts were turned on.

It merely tickled the beast. Jumbo II was unharnessed and taken back to his home in the Midway. Explanations made by the electricians were that the elephant's hide had the resistance of rubber and formed a non-conductor impervious to electricity. Others said the voltage was not sufficient.

"The white elephant campaign in the '80s was about the fiercest bit of circus rivalry I was ever mixed up in," he continued. "The Barnum show was the first to get one of the brutes. Their agent bought him from King Theebaw, the erratic sovereign of Burmah. The elephant was not white, but a leprous-looking shade of flesh color. It was really the first time one of these Albinos had ever been brought out of Asia. All that the king had done in the extravagant execution of his autocratic power was as nothing compared to the sale of the white elephant, and his subjects were furious. You see, the white elephant is a sacred emblem. It is addressed as 'Lord of Lords.' Priests prostrate themselves as it passes by and all the honors of worship are paid to it. A noble of high rank has to be its chamberlain. Its retinue is fit for a prince of the blood royal. Sickness in the sacred animal is ominous of coming evil. Its demeanor and gestures afford auguries, auspicious or sinister. For three years the Barnum white elephant made a lot of money for the show. Crowds flocked to see it, serene and placid and gently fanning itself with its wide ears, under a large Japanese parasol, native keepers meanwhile playing their queer musical instruments."

HOW TO BE A GUEST IN AN
ENGLISH COUNTRY HOME

MRS. M. L. RAYNE, *GEMS OF DEPORTMENT* (1881)

❧ ❧

A FAMOUS writer who visited our country several years ago, says the "American Queen," wrote a book about us, in which he declared that while an American knew how to be a host he did not yet understand the propriety of being a guest. It is probably quite true than an American did not in former years understand the severe etiquette which reigns in an English country-house. There the guests are expected to come at the hour invited, neither sooner nor later, and to leave precisely at the time when their term of invitation expires. It will be remembered that on the recent occasion of a tour around the world by a distinguished American general, he arrived at Windsor Castle, where he was an invited guest, some hours earlier than he was expected. There was no one to receive the company of foreigners. The queen was out riding with her daughter Beatrice, and never for a moment anticipating the arrival of her guests before the time specified in the note of invitation, had left no direction about receiving them at the Castle; and the court journal announced Her Majesty as looking "cross and sun-burned," when she alighted at her own doors, and found the guests whom she intended to honor seated stiffly in a reception room.

The reason of this English system of notifying guests of their expected stay and departure is this: A number of guests are invited with a certain formality for three days, and another company for the ensuing three days, which invitation is always so accurate that it specifies even if the guest is to leave by the "eleven train" or the "one train," as they express it in England. The great house is thus filled with a se-

· 8 ·

ries of congenial guests from the 1st of September, when the shooting begins, until after Christmas. The leisure man who is a good story-teller, can sing a song, or act in private theatricals, is much in demand; and on the events of these country visits hang most of the incidents of the modern society novel. Dickens described the less stately hospitality of the English country squire in his "Christmas at the Wardles," where the

renowned Pickwick Club spent, perhaps, the most jolly week of which we have any account in modern literature.

But even jolly Mr. Wardle, or the class which he is made to represent, would be particular as to a certain etiquette. Mr. Wardle would expect all his guests to arrive at the hour which he had named, and to be punctual at dinner.

It would be better for us in this country if we were as particular about the duties of a guest. We are too apt to suit our own convenience about going to see our friends; and, trusting to that boundless American hospitality, we decline an invitation for the 6th, saying we can come on the 9th of the month, which is not in accordance with the etiquette of the occasion, since we should either go on the 6th or not at all. We should also ask our host to define the limits of our stay, so that we may not exhaust our welcome. The terms of an American invitation are hospitably vague: "Come when you can, and stay as long as you like"— a social word kindness, at variance with the rules of etiquette.

"Welcome the coming, speed the parting guest," is found in the Arabian as well as in the Latin poets. The Arab goes further: "He who tastes my salt is sacred. Neither I nor my household shall attack him, nor shall one word be said against him." One phrase is worthy of particular study: "Nor shall one word be said against him"; no stabs in the back as he goes his way. Unless a guest has been publicly objectionable, it is in the worst possible taste to criticize him after he is gone. He has come to you at your own invitation; he has stayed at your house at your request; he has come as to an altar of safety, an ark of refuge, to your friendly roof. Your kind welcome has unlocked his reserve. He has spoken freely, laid off his armor, felt that he was in the presence of friends. If, in so doing, you have discovered in him a weak spot, be

lips of a guest. "Whose bread I have eaten, he is henceforth a brother," is another fine Arab proverb, worthy of being engraved on all our walls.

Much harm is done by the gadding and gossiping visitor through the thoughtless habit of telling of the manner of life, of the faults, quarrels, or shortcomings of the family under whose roof the

careful how you attack it. The intimate unreserve of your fireside should be respected. And upon the guest an equal, nay, a superior, conscientiousness should rest as to any revelation of what particular secrets she may discover while he is a visitor. No man or woman should go from house to house bearing tales, and spreading foolish and injurious reports or scandal. No stories of the weakness of this member of the family or the eccentricities of that one should ever be heard from the

careless talker has been admitted. Even much talk of their habits and ways is in bad taste. Speak always well of your entertainers, but say little of their domestic life. Do not violate the sanctity of that fireside treat whose roof-tree has sheltered you. Such is the true old Anglo-Saxon idea of the duty of a guest. It holds well today. We can not improve upon it.

Manifest etiquette demands that, once in your friend's house, you inform yourself as to the hours and customs, and conform exactly. Breakfast is an informal meal, and many large houses now allow their guests to take a cup of tea or coffee in their own room, with a slice of toast and an egg, and to not regularly breakfast until eleven or twelve o'clock, as the French do. But if it is the order of the house to have early breakfast, and the hostess says, "We shall expect you at the breakfast-table at eight o'clock," the guest is bound to obey.

An American breakfast, though delicious, is quite too elaborate to begin the day on. We should be better for the more delicate morning meal of the Swiss people—a roll and a cup of café-au-lait.

As guests, we are bound to make ourselves as agreeable as possible. No little tempers, no sour looks, no adverse opinions, no unpleasant criticisms, should ever fall from the lips of a guest. The most disagreeable of all circumstances should find a guest firmly good-tempered. We are not asked to our friend's house to show our little tempers. Never abuse the weather or the family dog. Although the long storm may seem tedious, the weather is, for the nonce, the prop-

erty of your host. Try in every way to counteract the external gloom by suggesting that you can get up tableaux, assist at private theatricals, or take a hand at whist or bezique, or join in any amusement which may be on the tapis. Pay especial attention to the wishes of your hostess, who is the queen of the castle. Be her dutiful subject.

The servants are always a tender point. No one, however judicious and kindly, can bear to have a servant spoken of with dislike. We are the servants of our servants in a measure, and their defects are our especial property. We are jealous of their good name, even if we are aware of their faults. We may like to find fault with them ourselves, but we do not intend that any one else shall.

Above all things, never join in when one member of the family has a difference with another. This is a sad breach of social and domestic etiquette, and one that is never tolerated. It is characteristic of weak and imperfect human nature that we can abuse our own with impunity, but no friend or acquaintance will be permitted to meddle. If it is a breach of etiquette in those whom we are visiting to wash their soiled linen in public, it is even more for us to make the offense more enormous by lending our aid and countenance. As for those who interfere in the domestic tiffs between husband and wife, history, poetry, and the drama have sufficiently elucidated their unhappy fate.

Never notice any omissions in the provisions made for the comfort of guests. "Fussing" is characteristic of American ladies, who spend so much more time within doors than their English sisters. If the guest-chamber lacks some comfort you have been accustomed to, say nothing about it unless it is indispensable, in which case it was probably an oversight. Never ask to have windows opened or closed, fires made, or lunches served. If your hostess has not made sufficient preparations for your comfort, cut your visit short, depart gracefully, and avoid her invitations in future; but keep your discomfiture locked in your own bosom.

The Arab law of hospitality is so noble, so comprehensive, so grand, that, although it transcends all social forms, we can use it to enforce the meaning of that law of etiquette and its vital spirit. Longfellow beautifully embodies an old-time castle of welcome in four lines in "The Old Clock on the Stairs":

In that mansion used to be
Free-hearted hospitality:
His great fires up the chimney
*   roared,*
The stranger feasted at his board.

There is another class of people who, with less money and living in a plain way, have none the less the great virtue of hospitality. They may be people of education, with fine aesthetic tastes, but are compelled to practice a severe economy. With only one servant, possibly not any, they will invite the one or two guests—dear friends, relatives, or those whom it is a pleasure to meet and entertain. The best bedroom is set in order; chickens are fed up and doomed to slaughter; early teas, to which neighbors are invited, are planned; and rides into pleasant nooks after Mayflowers, Autumn leaves, or whatever the attraction of the season may be, are set down for the visitor's benefit. The hostess in this case does every thing at a sacrifice of self, and her visitors should not stay long enough to wear her out. Perhaps she is one of that numerous class of women who has worked hard in her home all Winter, and is expected to entertain city friends all Summer. Perhaps she is married to one of the sons who has kept the old home. All the brothers, with their troops of children, must come back to the old shade-trees and meadows for a quiet rest. Perhaps they have no special love for the hostess who presides over the old-time house; but it is such a convenient thing to have a place to visit where there is fresh air, pure milk, plenty of good fruit, and no bills to pay. Ten to one the wife in the country is more worn than her city relatives, and is in no wise able to bear the extra care or the additional cooking; for, by force of circumstances, she has been dressmaker, milliner, and servant. May be, in her large family, the whole year through she has turned dresses wrong side out and up side down. She has made every dollar go its farthest. And now her visitors have come to take up all her self-sacrifice has saved. It might have been a pleasure to entertain them for a week; but when they remain six weeks or two months the case is different. We once heard a gentleman remark that he could say all the new things he had to say to visitors in one day; and, as a rule, we quite agree with him. Of course, one has congenial friends, whom it is a pleasure to see much and often; but too many so-called friends are persons who are serving their own convenience and outraging the laws of hospitality—persons who never offer a helping hand, and seem oblivious that everything is done for them by their entertainers. Never make a Summer visit at the expense of anybody's comfort.

A word about children visiting. Do not let them run over everybody, and monopolize every room. If they can not have a good time without destroying the comfort of a household, put them to bed, and keep them there, until they promise to amuse themselves in a rational manner. Children can be the most despotic little tyrants, as well as the sweetest of cherubs. They need a wholesome restraining, as much for their own good as for the happiness of older people.

Table Manners

A well-known writer on society topics says: Among the most trust-

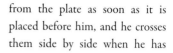

worthy tests of good home training is placed that of table manners; and no individual can hope to acquire and to keep them who knows any difference in them, when in the privacy of the family circle, or in company. The properly trained youth does not annoy those next to whom he sits by fidgeting in his chair, moving his feet, playing with his bread, or with any of the table equipage. Neither does he chew his food with his mouth open, talk with it in his mouth, or make any of those noises in eating which are the characteristics of vulgarity. His food is not conveyed in too large or too small portions to his mouth; he neither holds his head as erect as though he had swallowed a ramrod, nor does he bury his face in his plate. He handles his knife and fork properly, and not overhanded, as a clown does; he removes them

from the plate as soon as it is placed before him, and he crosses them side by side when he has

finished, and not before, as this is the signal which a well-drilled butler observes for removing the plate. He does not leave his coffee-spoon or tea-spoon in his cup. He avoids using his handkerchief unnecessarily, or disgusting those at table with a trumpet-like performance with it. He does not converse in a loud tone, nor indulge in uproarious laughter.

If he breaks anything, he is not profuse in his apologies, but shows his regret in his face and manner, rather than in words. Some writer has said: "As it is ill-mannered to express too much regret, so it is the essence of rudeness not to make an apology." Titlebus Titmouse, when he broke a glass, assured his host that he would replace it with the best in London. This was rather too practical a form of showing his sincerity.

The well-bred man breaks his

bread instead of cutting it, taking care not to crumble it in a slovenly way. He does not hesitate to pass

any course of which he does not wish to partake, instead of playing with it, as a writer on table etiquette advises. He swallows his food before he leaves the table, and sees no occasion for astonishment because eating on the street is forbidden. All the details of good breeding are as familiar to him as his alphabet, and he has been taught to think that attention in small things is the true sign of a great mind, and that he who can in necessity consider the smallest can also compass the largest subjects.

How to Ride a High Wheeler

Timsley Brothers, *Bicycling* (1879)

❧ ❧

Riding and Learning to Ride

An ounce of knowledge is worth a ton of theory, and there is no royal road to bicycle riding any more than there is to the attainment of any other desirable object. Cases are on record of persons learning the art in an incredibly short space of time, and we were informed the other day of an instance of a rider who purchased a machine at a large provincial factory, and after being shown simply how to mount, actually rode away on it, without any previous practice. Such instances are however extremely rare, and must not be allowed to mislead. Patient persevering practice is required to become a proficient and elegant bicyclist.

In the choice of a bicycle it is undoubtedly the truest economy to purchase only the best quality, and that from a well-known manufacturer, whose reputation is the buyer's best safeguard for the superiority of the machine he sells.

For if it be considered that a bicycle, which must bear the wear and tear of all kinds of roads, and carry a weight of ten to fourteen stone at a rate of twelve to fifteen miles an hour, for days together if necessary, weighs only forty-five pounds, it will be at once conceded that not only must it be made of the very best materials which money can buy, but that its construction demands also the finest mechanical skill and ability which can be bestowed upon it.

Second rate material, and second rate labor, are not only absolutely unreliable, but perilous to life and limb. This warning cannot be too strenuously enforced.

A high class bicycle is not expensive beyond the first outlay; it may be ridden daily, and will last for years if only ordinary attention be paid to keeping the wearing parts well cleaned and lubricated with the best sperm oil. Even should a casualty occur, in most cases the necessary repairs and adjustments can be done at a trifling cost.

By way of illustration, we heard the other day of an overthrown bicycle being run over by a dray, at Aldershot, all the wheels of which passed over it; nevertheless the rider was run down by a van belonging to a menagerie, and although the wheel was knocked into the shape of a badly executed figure eight, no single spoke, screw, spring, or bearing was broken, and in a few hours the machine was made as efficient as before. These were high-class bicycles. On the other hand, you may, during the season, read almost weekly, in the Field, of tourists whose journeys have been delayed, or altogether abandoned, through such mishaps as "broken backbone," "broken spokes," and we have even seen "broken tires." And to such reports you see almost invariably attached the name of a second-class maker.

The best known makers are Sparrow, of London, Keen, of Sur-

biton, Timerlake, of Maidenhead, Humber, of Nottingham, and The Coventry Machinists' Company, of Coventry; the latter are the oldest established and by far the largest makers in the country, if indeed their factory and plant be not the largest in the world for the manufacture of bicycles.

It is well for the beginner not to be too ambitious about the size of the driving-wheel; confidence is more certainly acquirable for the largest possible radius the rider's length of leg can compass, for the sake of the speed thereby to be obtained without any greater labor.

Where practicable, it is very advisable to learn on a small wooden machine, and we say *experto crede*, this will not be injured in appearance by the few harmless falls that the tyro generally has to take in the beginning, with the best grace he may. Decidedly the better way in the first instance is to obtain the assistance of a friend, and this there can be little difficulty in doing. The knack of *balancing* is really all there is to be actually learned, the rest comes by practice, and that gives the confidence which enables riders to do the great things in the way of speed and distance that the equestrian may sigh for in vain.

On a gentle slope and on a machine with a small wheel, you may then, alone if necessary, take your seat, and proceed, grasping the handle, not too tightly but *never leaning on it*, and if your machine be low enough for your feet to just touch the ground, so much the better. If you find the balance

have learned all that a bicyclist needs by way of precept. The next thing is to accustom the feet and legs to the motion of the pedals, in order to do which, it is necessary to place the feet lightly on them, allowing the motion of the machine to carry them round.

Do not attempt to exert any pressure on the pedals until you become thoroughly accustomed to

LE BICYCLE DE 3 METRES
DE RENARD (1878)

MOUNTING

difficult to acquire on starting, and that the machine has an inclination to fall, a mere touch with the toe, on the ground, on whichever side the machine is falling, will right you again. The pedals must not be used in the first essays, the impetus given by the incline being sufficient to move the machine with quite enough velocity for you to learn to balance and steer. When you have mastered this, you

their motion. As your feet are now employed and cannot touch the ground to restore equilibrium, if you experience a tendency to fall, bear in mind, *to turn the wheel gently and without the slightest jerk in the direction the bicycle is falling.* This is the whole secret of success in bicycle riding, and cannot be too attentively observed. To a finished rider this motion is an instinct, but, until you arrive at this stage of perfection, it will need to be carefully remembered and practiced. If you turn the wheel in the opposite direction you will assuredly fall. We have heard many people say, "Why! I should have turned the wheel just the opposite way!" but we repeat this is an error, it must be turned in the direction in which you have a tendency to fall, and the more skillfully you bring the rule into practice, the more certain and speedy will be your progress. After a little experience in riding, so that you have become somewhat accustomed to the balance and the pedals, you may endeavor to mount. This, it is advisable, should be first attempted from some support, such as a wall or post, and not by the step. You will by this means gradually acquire the confidence necessary to mount and also dismount by means of the step in the proper manner. To mount by a wall, you place the machine in a nearly upright position against it, placing the pedal that is away from the wall just past the top of the throw. This is to ensure your getting a good start with your outside foot. Mount your machine and take hold of the outside handle, but

with the other hand steady yourself against the wall, gently bringing the machine into a perpendicular position. As soon as it has attained this, push your outside pedal downwards, this will give you the requisite start and enable you to bring your other foot into use. This way of mounting will an-

THE LEG-REST—DOWN-HILL

swer your purpose until you have arrived at some proficiency as a rider; you may then endeavor to do so in the ordinary way, by means of the step. To do this, take the machine by both handles, place the left toe upon the step, and, taking two or three short hops to get a little "way" on the machine, raise yourself on the step and drop into the saddle. In learning, it is always best to do this on a gentle descent; it is also desirable, in order to avoid a fall, to keep the wheel turned about two inches out of the perpendicular and towards you, so that, in the event of your not succeeding in reaching the saddle at the first attempt, you will drop on the side you started from.

It is quite impossible to state arbitrarily how long this state of pupilage will last. No two riders, on comparing notes, ever find their experiences coincident. We can only counsel patience and resolution, and give the assurance that bicycling is not so difficult after all, and that success is within easy reach of all who persevere; a few hours being generally enough to learn each successive stage on the way to complete mastery over the machine. Frequent practice (but not by exhaustive spells of work) is of the greatest importance; and a sure aid to the maintenance of self-possession is to bear continually in mind the few precepts we venture to give. Of course, an impending fall, if not checked by gently and slightly turning the front wheel in the direction you are falling, as previously suggested, must be submitted to, and rendered as little unpleasant as possible; we therefore counsel the rider to yield to the machine if it does not immediately right itself on the action of the handle, and waiting till it has nearly reached the ground, then throw out the leg. The acquisition of a graceful and easy seat, and the economy of your motive power, are the next two things to be striven for. Avoid stiffness, whether in the joints of the legs and arms, or in the pose of the body, and do not attempt to sit rigidly upright with military exactness. The act of dismounting being exactly the converse of mounting, it is scarcely necessary to say more than that the left toe should be accustomed to seek the step and find it with ease, whereupon the rider can drop lightly on the ground on his right foot, not relinquishing his hold of the machine handle until he is safe on terra firma. Experienced riders generally acquire the habit of descending without using the step, and leave the machine from the treadle direct, or by throwing the left leg over the handle. A tyro should never attempt this.

The use of the leg-rest permits the rider, on descending hills, to rest from the labor of working the treadles, and merely steer his course with the handle.

Acrobatic performances, such as riding side-saddle fashion and standing on the seat like a circus-rider, are occasionally to be seen. The learner should never attempt anything of the sort until his mastery over the machine is quite perfect; even then he will do well to avoid these displays, and give his attention to the increase of his speed of traveling.

Bicycling has many advantages for all classes: in addition to its acknowledged utility to country clergymen and doctors, road-surveyors, and others who have long rounds to perform, and who are so rapidly adopting the machines, we are glad to add the testimony of a very hard-worked body of men, the letter-carriers, who, with this aid to locomotion, can perform their "weary round" of ten or twenty miles with scarcely any fatigue. The healthiness of the exercise has never been questioned; the difficulties of learning are not greater than those of horse-riding, skating, or swimming, and the acquisition places a man of ordinary strength in a position equal—nay,

superior to—the trained professional jockey, or pedestrian, inasmuch as he has his motive power contained within himself, and that power is augmented, as well as

DISMOUNTING

economized, by the improved mechanism of the bicycle of today. If bicycling continues to increase in popularity as it is increasing, Mr. Disraeli's lament last session, that, "the British race is in a state of physical decline," may well be withdrawn. There is no exercise so salutary for the development of the muscles of arms, legs, and back, and the bicyclists may well take for their own the trite motto, *Vires acqvirit evndo*.

Dress for Bicycling

For racing, the best dress is that usually worn by runners, consisting of a thin jersey, with knickerbockers, or trousers cut to the knee, made of silk, or some such light material.

The tourist has to take into consideration what is most useful and comfortable for a long ride, as well as what is least likely to hamper his movements. For a long journey, riders will find knickerbockers more comfortable than trousers and gaiters. A flannel shirt and a short yachting coat will complete the costume (serge is the best wearing material), though a mackintosh strapped to the machine is indispensable. A light gun or fishing-rod can be tied along the spring, as well as a bag containing sponge, brushes, etc. Thus equipped, a rider may travel for days among the Highlands of Scotland, or through the wildest parts of Ireland.

FALLING

IF ATTACKED BY A BULL

LT. COL. BARON DE BERENGER, *HELPS & HINTS* (1835)

❧ ❦

BULLS, *cows, deer,* and *horned animals, generally* charge with as much stupidity as desperation; you may *avoid* or even *avert* their horns, *the first by activity and judgment,* the second by a *sharp cut* at the tip of the horn, which, owing to the force applied to the extremity of a lever, jars and hurts them, but *it requires great expertness and decision*; so far you *may* succeed, but you cannot resist, much less overcome, the weight and impetus of their charge: a *winding* run, with *many* and *sudden turns* will serve you, sometimes a coat, a hat—nay, even and particularly a *red* handkerchief, *dropped in your flight*, will *arrest* the attention of the animal, *to give you time to gain ground*, whilst it is goring or smelling *what* you have thrown before it; but the *best* way is, to *make for a large tree*, if one is near, in order to stand closely *before* it, and even to irritate the animal to a charge, thereupon nimbly to *slip on one side and behind the tree*, which, receiving the charge, most likely will fling the assailant down, with the shock returned upon itself. I have been saved in a similar way from the fury of a bull, by making towards and placing myself before the wall of Bellsize park, for, as the bull *dropped his head*! And *charged*!! I made *a side leap of six feet and more*, to scramble away as fast as I could; but my fear was quite unnecessary, for, having broken one of his horns, and stunned himself otherwise, I left him laying with his tongue out and motionless; whether he recovered, or paid the forfeit of his life for his unprovoked malice, I had neither curiosity nor relish to ascertain, for he had given me a *long* and *distressing* heat to reach this wall, and which, by zig-zags only, I effected; for he

had more speed than myself, although then I was *rather* a superior runner, but, by overshooting the turn at each zig-zag, *he* lost ground; had he not been so very fast, I might have resorted to *another* mode, that of *taking off my coat, and of throwing it over his horns*: if ever you do the latter, you must not expect to *wear* it again, nor should I advise its use if you have *any* valuable in the pockets. Some recommend that you should *leap over the bull's lowered head on to his back*: it may do, *if* you can make *sure* of not *falling* off, for slip off you must of course; but, like hitting the beast *a sharp blow across the forelegs*, it will do, and is an excellent application of gymnastics, provided you can make *sure*, for *if you fail you are lost*, or you are at his mercy at any rate. It is something like *laying down*, although not quite so tame, for that answers

sometimes, that is, as a *last resort*, and provided you *lay motionless*; and then you should hold your breath, and also keep *your face towards the ground*. Make up your mind of being not only well *smelled over*, by a bull or ox, but also *turned over with the horns*, and *trampled upon*, and, *if that is all*, you may get up contented, when he is *out of sight*, for he may watch you suspiciously and cunningly; but with a *wild boar*, and certainly *not* with a *stag*, especially a red one, I should *not like to experimentalize in this way*, although I have heard it recommended: *Most* of the *other methods may be found useful with these animals, as well as with oxen and bulls, but, like cows, most of these keep their eyes open when they charge, whilst a bull or an ox shuts them, an intimation you ought not to forget!*

HOW TO BUY AN ELEPHANT

And 38 Other Things You Never Knew

You Wanted to Know!

WHOM & WHEN TO MARRY

HENRY DAVENPORT NORTHRUP, *THE HOME EDUCATOR* (1893)

❧ ❧

A FAMILY is a great affair. As a commodity, a production, a life-work, an achievement, it has no peers. Its power over man is supreme. As it is, so is all else human. As a "speculation," a "venture," if well conducted, it is the most "paying enterprise," yields better "dividends," and is every way more "profitable" than any other "line of business" in which mortals can "invest." Those who possess the capital should procure a "roundtrip" ticket for this matrimonial excursion. It will take you around and through the world in better style, and show you finer "prospects" than any other.

Where can men learn how a family should be founded and conducted? Strange that, whilst every other department of science has been explored, family science remains still enshrouded in Egyptian darkness. Scholars, where have you been groping, that you have not discovered this field of human research? Writers, where have been your pens? Clergymen, where are your eyes and tongues that you thus ignore it?

Self-preparation is first, just as preparing the ground is the first step towards obtaining a crop; and the next, selection of a right sexual mate; and this chapter has for its object to show how to take this step just right.

Love has its natural period, and prospers better when it is observed. And it has but one right time, which is exactly right, because appointed by Nature. She is perfect, so are all her works; her love-works included. To a complete love, this observance of her natural times and seasons is indispensable. True, though one may make an excellent crop of cotton or corn, even if planted out of time, yet how much better that same crop if planted when Nature ordains? Then, when is Nature's best time for planting the seeds of love?

The sexual function matures later than the digestive or muscular; because its earlier development would be useless, yet retard growth. Boys and girls like each other some, but how much stronger is appetite than love, and love years after than at puberty? The sexuality slumbers on till quickened by puberty, which re-increases it till eighteen or twenty, when the body is well grown and consolidated; bones become dense, and their gristly joints hardened up; muscles full-sized and tort; and mental faculties fully established. Love now begins to assert sovereign control. No puppy love, no "juvenile and tender" fancy, but a deep, strong, all-controlling and mature affection inspires and electrifies the whole being, and furnishes and inhabits the human structure, taking that helm which governs every part.

Previous starvation also often induces both sudden and premature love. If boys were duly loved and fondled by mother and aunt, and girls similarly by father and uncles, and if this faculty were duly cultivated in lads, lasses, and young folks, this, its partial exercise, would so far satisfy it in the bud as to hold back love proper a year or two longer, and mitigate its violence; whereas its juvenile suppression renders it so ravenous that it greedily devours whatever food is offered. Elders, consider this point, and compare it with your experience.

Intellect should govern every life movement, and especially marriage. This step is too eventful to be taken by giddy youth. Females just begin to come to their senses at sixteen, and males about eighteen, some sooner, according as they ripen earlier or later, yet it then requires a year or two for both the love instinct and judgment to become sufficiently matured to consummate this eventful choice. The more so since earlier fancies change. One who might exactly suit at sixteen, might not at twenty; but one who is all right at twenty, will please always; because the love basis is now fully established for life; which is rarely the case before seventeen.

Differences of Age

The love of an elderly man for a girl is more parental than conjugal; while hers for him is like that of a daughter for a father, rather than wife for husband. He loves her as a pet, and therefore his inferior, instead of as a woman; and is compelled to look down upon her as inexperienced, below him in judgment, too often impulsive and unwise; which obliges him to make too many allowances to be compatible with a genuine union. And she is compelled to look up to him more as one to be reverenced, perhaps feared, and as more good and wise than companionable. Their ideas and feelings must necessarily be dissimilar. He may indeed pet, flatter, and indulge her as he would a grown daughter, and appreciate her artless innocence and girlish light-heartedness; yet all this is not genuine masculine and feminine love; nor can she exert over him the influence every man requires from his wife.

All girls should aught play, be juvenile, and mingle in young society, and an elderly husband might not want to go to as many parties as his girl-wife. Of course she must stifle her love of company, or else be escorted by a younger, perhaps therefore more sympathetic beau, who must play the agreeable, whisper pleasant things, perhaps expressions of love, in her willing ear, while she prefers the young beau, and is quite liable to love her hus-

CHAUNCEY M. DEPEW—STRONG, COMPACT BODY; LARGE PERCEPTIVE FACULTIES AND LANGUAGE; FINE SOCIAL QUALITIES, ORATORICAL GIFTS AND BUSINESS CAPACITIES.

band rather as a father, yet another as a lover. At least those elderly men who marry girls must keep only half an eye half open, and see little even with that. Not that their young consorts are faithless, but that they are exposed to temptation.

A young woman deficient in amativeness naturally gravitates

towards elderly men; because their greater age has put theirs on about the same plane with hers. Such girls, therefore, greatly prefer men from twenty to thirty years their seniors. In such cases her preferences may be safely trusted.

The Stylish Woman

Style is desirable, if well sustained and does not degenerate into ostentation. Does she appear well in company? Can you introduce her properly to your old comrades as your beau-ideal? A pleasing, "taking," attractive address which combines grace with elegance, and charms while it sways, is a great recommendation. Not that we attempt to analyze good manners, but only call attention to them as very expressive of character; yet affected artificiality, a constrained aping of gentility, indicates a make-believe outside appearance, and want of genuineness; while a natural, unaffected simplicity in walk, speech, and manners betokens a truthfulness to nature every way desirable.

Dandyism, foppery, broadcloth, ladies, must not be allowed to outweigh true manliness of manner, though perhaps eclipsed by bashfulness or awkwardness. Has he the rudiments of a good address? Not is he, but can he become, polished? Often internal coarseness assumes a sugar-coated, genteel impudence which provokes laughter, and passes off for the moment, yet discloses long ears. Look below the surface. Women generally overrate forward, but greatly underrate diffident young men. Undue forwardness discloses a familiarity which springs, if not from contempt of the sex, at least a want of due respect for it; while awkwardness often originates in that exalted worship of it which is indispensable in a husband.

The expression of talents and worth stands second only to their possession. Conversational, speaking, and writing talent can hardly be overrated, yet is almost wholly overlooked. Its manifestation, in whichever form, justly challenges the admiration of the world, past and present, savage and civilized, learned and illiterate; yet wherein does conversational eloquence differ from forensix, except in the number of its listeners? Is it not as admirable in the cottage as on the rostrum? Hence, what are his talents for expressing himself? What of her conversational powers? These are paramount questions, and the answers most significant.

Artificial Ninnies

If a plain girl's ideas flow readily, and she clothes them in appropriate and beautiful language, this gift recommends her more than all the boarding-school artificialities and millinery she can exhibit. Does she warm up with her subject, and impart to it a glow, an interest, which delights and inspires? Does she choose words which express her precise meaning, and begin her sentences at the right end; or does she bungle both? Is she grammatical; or does she murder the "King's English"? Not "Can she speak French," but can she talk elegantly? It matters little whether she has studied grammar, for natural conversational talent will evince itself irrespective of educational aids, which of course help. Does she spoil a good story by telling it badly, or so tell every one as to make its point of application emphatic? Is she suggestive? Does she make you think and feel as she converses?

Many object to long female tongues, as given to scandal; whereas, whether one talks well or ill has absolutely nothing to do with backbiting. Scandal is consequent on a malevolent spirit, not on a "long tongue." One may say a little, but misrepresent that; or talk much, yet give a true version. Neglect those girls who, looking through inverted glasses, always represent things as worse than they really are; but patronize pleased and hopeful ones who paint whatever they attempt to say or do in beautiful, handsome colors, and regard things favorably.

Sexuality, normal and abundant, alone creates whatever is manly and womanly; attracts and is attracted, loves and awakens love, inspirits and inspirited, fuses and is fused, molds and is molded, and both confers life and predetermines its amount. All other conjugal prerequisites sink into insignificance when compared with this, because it is the summary and embodiment of all; that which is to all what lime is to mortar, or tendon to muscle. The answer to the questions, "How much mental and physical manhood has this beau as compared with that? How much of a female is this woman as compared with that?" should mainly determine the choice. "Which is the most magnetic, and capable of the deepest, completest devotion, will inspire the most love in me, and call out my manly affections and attributes?" is a man's great practical inquiry; while a woman's should be, "Which is truest to masculine nature, and will bestow the most on me?" not which is the most polite or spruce?

Do not choose one too good, or too far above, for yourself, lest the inferior, by dissatisfying the superior, breed those discords which are worse than mutual satisfaction with those not so highly organized. Don't be too particular; for you might go farther and fare worse. As far as you yourself are faulty, you should put up with faults. Don't cheat a consort by getting one much better than you can give. We are not in heaven yet, and must put up with their imperfections, and instead of grumbling at them be glad they are no worse; remembering that a faulty one is a great deal better than none.

Likes and Dislikes

Some men like large, others small, and still others medium-sized women; some this complexion, which is odious to others; and thus of all the other physical qualities. One woman admires, another dislikes, the very same men and attributes. One can hardly tolerate what perfectly fascinates another; and yet both are intelligent, and judge correctly and alike in other respects.

Thus, that consumptive, who, by marrying one who is consumptive, "foreordains" the consumption and death of his children, whereas, by marrying one well vitalized, he might have secured robust offspring, is most guilty for this consumptive taint; and for not entailing robustness.

What if he is honest, kind, devout, fatherly, and all that, yet did he not cause their death? And is not causing it by hereditary entailment as wicked as by poison?

Again you say, "For young people to thus canvass each other's parental qualities before or during courtship, is at least indelicate, if not improper."

Is Nature "improper"? Is rearing children "indelicate?" Is providing for good children any more "immodest" than for poor? All depends on the manner, nothing on the fact. Nature makes, and therefore you should make, children the specific object of all marriage. If this is "indelicate," then is being a male or female improper, and courting, loving, marrying, and bearing children, immodest? She who looks this only legitimate end of marriage fully in its philosophic face will make an immeasurably better wife and mother than she could possibly make if her "mock-modesty" ignored it. Those too delicate to ascertain their parental adaptations to each other are but mockish prudes, and most indelicate. Those whose modesty ignores this kind of information, are quite too modest to marry or bear children at all; and to be consistent, should never love, or look at the other sex, or even be sexed; and are welcome to the result of their fastidiousness.

Every stage of reproduction, from the first dawnings of love, through selection, marriage, paternity, and maternity, is no more indelicate, in itself, than sleeping, except that "as a man thinketh in his heart so is he." No; so choosing, loving, and marrying as to produce magnificent children, is modest; while marrying for any other motive is most decidedly "immodest."

You, young, pure, wholesome girl, affectionate, bright, and domestic in your tastes, should not marry a man who has bad habits, or is ever likely to have them. Heaven forbid that you should ever be the wife of a dissipated husband.

Persons to Be Avoided

You should not receive the attentions of a thin, sallow-faced, sour dyspeptic. His foul stomach will kill the health of yours: I mean that by his gloomy, draggy, low vitality and cheerless, dismal disposition, he will drive you to dyspepsia or something worse, if there is anything worse, and you will find that you might as well go and be a nurse in a hospital, or live in a graveyard, as to attempt to extract comfort and happiness from your alliance with such a living corpse. Seek a man with good digestion—round, full, ruddy—if you can find him, genial, as health is almost sure to be, a live man, not a half dead one. And if you are a dyspeptic, you certainly don't want a dyspeptic husband. I would rather have a pocketbook as flat as the traditional pan-cake than to have a caved-in stomach.

Young lady, do not marry a mean, miserly man. You might almost as well marry a spendthrift, for in either case you will be lucky if you ever get hold of any money. Men don't wear hair-pins, nor feathers, nor ribbons, nor lace and fringes, and a close-fisted, narrow miserly man will begrudge every penny you spend. He will tie up his money in an old stocking, and you can go without stockings.

And you, young man, look out whom you marry. A woman may be of such an age that she is called an "old maid," yet she may be twenty-five years younger in heart and hope, courage and industry, than that girl only twenty years old. That girl of twenty may be the old maid—crabbed, sour, exacting, stiff—a creature to be avoided— her mouth eternally drawn down and her nose turned up—keep clear of her! Give her a wide berth—in fact, let her have it all to herself. She will be so prim that neither anybody or anything will suit her. She will freeze you in July.

She is an icicle with a female hat on.

To whom is such a person suited? Nobody. Neither is the mean man, nor the pale dyspeptic, nor the dissipated wretch whose hat and windows have holes in them big enough to defy ever being stuffed or mended.

If either loves to ride fast, and the other slow, how can they possibly ride together without making one or the other unhappy?

When one loves dress, parties, style, gaiety, or fashion, and the other considers them foolish, or regards them with aversion, can they be as happy in each other, and therefore love each other as well if both like or disliked the same things? If both take delight in pursuing the same studies together, will not this mutual delight render them much happier in each other, and therefore more affectionate, than if one liked but the other disliked the same books? Did not Milton's conjugal difficulty grow out of dis-similarity? He was talented, philosophical, poetical; but his wife despised what he liked, and liked those gaieties which he condemned.

How often are a strong, robust,

CRABBED OLD MAID

herit his powerful animal organism, along with her exquisite taste and moral tone; and are therefore far better than if both parents were powerfully animalized, or both exquisitely emotional.

Great sizes, along with extreme susceptibility, expend too much power, and hence should intermarry with those at least good-sized, in order to balance their undue ardor with the other's coolness and power. If escorting a woman of more commanding appearance than himself should mortify a small man, he should feel proud that he could win one his physical superior, and had better mortify himself a little, than his

coarse, shaggy-locked, red-faced, powerful man, and most exquisitely susceptible, fine-grained, delicate, refined, and pure-minded woman, drawn together? One would think her delicacy would revolt at his coarseness, and his power despise her exquisiteness. What attracts them? Her need of animality. By presupposition her delicate organism has about exhausted her sparse fund of vitality, so that she is perishing for want of this first requisite of life, and naturally gravitates to one who emanates sufficient animal magnetism to support both; so that she literally lives on his surplus animal warmth and vitality, he being all the better for this draft while she pays him back by refining and elevating him; and their children in-

MEAN OLD MISER

children always. Yet she need not exceed him much in stature, especially if prominent-featured and large framed; for a good-sized woman is but little larger than a small-sized man. Yet the wife of a large man really should have a large mouth, and a tough, enduring temperament, with good muscles.

Tom Thumb, a dwarf himself, confessed to a most marked preference for good-sized women; and

AMELIA RIVES CHANLER—
NERVOUS, INTELLECTUAL TEM-
PERAMENT; BRILLIANT MIND,
PREDOMINATING OVER BODY;
LACKING IN PHYSICAL BREADTH
AND ROBUSTNESS.

his child by his dwarf wife weighed only two pounds at birth, lingered, and died.

"Little folks" must not marry little, unless they are willing to have still smaller children; but must marry good-sized, and their children will be medium.

Rev. Dr. Bartoll, an excellent authority, says: "If we would have no monsters about us, let not idiots or insane pair, or scrofulous or consumptives, those soaked in alcohol or conceived in lust, entering the world diseased in body or mind, or overweighed with any propensity or passion, be allowed to marry, any more than we would have a nursery for wolves and bears, or cultivate poisonous ivy, deadly night-shade, or apple-fern in the enclosures of our houses, our yards and fields. Society, by righteous custom, if not by statute law, has a right to prevent, to forbid the multiplication of monstrous specimens of humanity.

But most who can, may multiply; because progeny is as natural a birthright as eating. All our faculties were created only to act. As a right to exercise lungs, stomach, muscles, eyes, etc., accompanies their bestowal; so a right to exercise every mental faculty inheres in their birthright possession. Shall human authority forbid what divine more than permits—imperiously commands, and even necessitates?

How can society prevent? Those interdicted would rebel, and seek clandestinely that intercourse forbidden them by law, and leave illegitimate issue if denied legitimate. Shall the law marry only those men and women sexually and morally vigorous, and emasculate all inferior boy babies? How would it be possible to draw the lines impartially as to who should and who should not suffer the surrender of these marital rights? Or what their rules of allowing and interdicting? The difficulties in the way of such a course are insurmountable.

God adjudicates this identical matter by His natural law, in rendering childless all who cannot have children much better than none.

Harlots rarely become mothers, because their depravities would make their issue worthless. Nature will not begin what she cannot consummate, provided she is allowed her own facilities, and generally interdicts parentage to those either too young, too old, too debilitated or diseased anywhere, or deformed, or depraved, to impart sufficient of all the human functions to enable their children, by a right hygiene, to live to a good age, and well worthy to inhabit her "premises." By this simple arrangement she forestalls all those diseases, deformities, and marked imperfections which

EDWARD BELLAMY—LARGE PERCEPTIVE FACULTIES; DEFECTIVE REASONING POWERS, YET BOLD IN CONCEPTIONS; STRONG INDIVIDUALITY, AND DISLIKES OPPOSITION; CELEBRATED AUTHOR.

would otherwise impair, if not spoil, universal humanity.

Certain Opposites Should Combine

Bright red hair should marry jet black, and jet black auburn, or bright red. And the more red-faced and bearded or impulsive a man, the more dark, calm, cool and quiet should his wife be; and vice versa. The florid should not marry the florid, but those who are dark in proportion as they themselves are light.

Red-whiskered men should marry brunettes but not blondes; the color of the whiskers being more determinate of the temperament than that of the hair.

The color of the eyes is still more important. Gray eyes must marry some other color, almost any other, except gray; and so of blue, dark, hazel, etc.

Those very fleshy should not marry those equally so, but those too spare and slim; and this is doubly true of females. A spare man is much better adapted to a fleshy woman than a round-favored man. Two who are short, thick-set, and stocky, should not unite in marriage, but should choose those differently constituted; but on no account one of their own make. And, in general, those predisposed to corpulence are therefore less inclined to marriage.

Those with little hair or beard should marry those whose hair is naturally abundant; still, those who once had plenty, but who have lost it, may marry for those who are either bald or have but little; for in this, as in all other cases, all depends on what one is by Nature, little on present states.

Those whose motive-temperament decidedly predominates, who are bony, only moderately fleshy, quite prominent-featured,

AN IDIOT—OFFSPRING OF TWO SLUGGISH PARENTS, BOTH WEAK MENTALLY AND PHYSICALLY.

Roman-nosed, and muscular, should not marry those similarly formed, but those either sanguine or nervous, or a compound of both; for being more strong than susceptible or emotional, they both require that their own emotions should be perpetually prompted by an emotional companion, and that their children also be endowed with the emotional from the other parent. That is, those who are cool should marry those who are impulsive and susceptible.

Small, nervous men must not marry little nervous or sanguine women, lest both they and their children have quite too much of the hot-headed and impulsive, and die suddenly. Generally, ladies who are small are therefore more

An Ignoramus—Low, narrow head; animal face; obstinate disposition; entirely unsuited to an educated, well endowed woman.

and one of his own tribe, and civilized with civilized, and one of their own or like mode of civilization. Even those of different nationalities will find their national differences a source of many more discords than concords, and should marry only when love is sufficiently strong to overrule this national antagonism.

eagerly sought than large. Of course this general fact has its exceptions. Some are small hereditarily, others rendered so by extra action in some form, over-study, over-work, or passional excitement; because during growth, their intense nervous systems consumed energy faster than their weak vital could manufacture it; which dwarfed their stature.

Conflicting beliefs can love each other when their sexual attraction is sufficient to overcome religious differences; yet religious harmony increases, and differences diminish, their natural assimilation. So great is this sexual attraction, that a savage man and civilized woman can live happily together; yet how much more cordially could savage live with savage,

"A Cold, Distant Man"

Lack of affection in both will render their marriage and offspring tame, even though both are talented and moral. At least one should be affectionate, better if both are; yet her lot is hard, who, with warm, gushing affection, is repulsed when she expresses it. She who dearly loves to be caressed and fondled, should be; and if she marries a cold, distant man, whose love is merely personal, she must expect to pine and starve, and dispense, during maternity, with that sympathy and tenderness so much needed.

Few are perfect, mentally and sentimentally; therefore most require to offset their excesses and defects by marrying those unlike themselves. They must be

MISMATED—BOTH NERVOUS, LEAN, IRRITABLE, DYSPEPTIC; CONSTANT FRICTIONS IN MARRIED LIFE, EACH EXASPERATING THE OTHER; NOT SUITED TO EACH OTHER; EACH SHOULD HAVE MARRIED ONE MORE ROBUST, PATIENT AND AMIABLE.

sufficiently alike, in the majority of their great outline characteristics, to fuse their differences; but since almost all have too much or little caution, kindness, selfishness, taste, justice, etc., most need to marry those unlike themselves, in one or more respects.

Men who love to command must be especially careful not to marry imperious, women's-rights women; while those who willingly "obey orders," need just such. Some men require a wife who shall take their part; yet all who do not need

strong-willed women should be careful how they marry them. Unless you love to be opposed, be careful not to marry one who often argues and talks back; for discussion before marriage becomes obstinacy after.

Two very beautiful persons rarely do or should marry; nor two extra homely. The fact is a little singular that very handsome women, who of course can have their pick, rarely marry good-looking men, but generally give preference to those who are homely; because that exquisiteness in which beauty originates, naturally blends with that power which accompanies huge noses, and disproportionate features.

Psyche loved Apollo desperately, says Mythology, on account of his beauty. Now this must have been purely imaginary. No woman thus beautiful ever loved a handsome man, if she could find any other. Psyche would naturally choose a man of talents rather than of a good physique; and a right homely and even awkward man need not fear a refusal, if he is only powerful, original, logical, and smart.

Rapid movers, speakers, laughers, etc., should marry those who are calm and deliberate, and impulsives those who are stoical; while those who are medium may marry those who are either or neither, as they prefer.

Masculine women, who inherit their father's looks, stature, appearance, and physique mainly, should give preference to men who take most after mother, physically, while women cast strongly after their mother, should marry those men in whom the masculine form and physiology superabound.

Noses indicate characters by indicating the organisms and temperaments. Accordingly, those noses especially marked either way, should marry those having opposite nasal characteristics. Roman noses are adapted to those which turn up, and pug noses, to those turning down; while straight noses may marry either.

Narrow nostrils indicate small lungs. Such are adapted to those with broad nostrils, which accompany large lungs and vital organs.

Two having fine soft hair and skin are not as well adapted in marriage as those having one the coarser, the other finer; lest their offspring should be too exquisitely

ANIMAL ORGANISM—
LOW INTELLECT; SENSUAL
FEATURES; BAD TEMPER;
TYPE OF HUMAN BRUTE.

organized for their strength; nor should two very coarse-haired, lest their children prove too coarse and animal; yet those whose hair and skin are average, may marry fine, or coarse, or medium.

A right mental adaptation is, however, as much more important than a right physical, as the transmission of the mind is than that of the body. Gender, too, inheres mainly in the mind. Then what laws govern mental affiliations?

The reserved or secretive should marry the frank. A cunning man cannot endure the least artifice in a wife. Those who are noncommittal must marry those who are demonstrative; else however much they may love, neither will feel sure as to the other's affections, and each will distrust the other, while their children will be deceitful. Those who are frank and confiding also need to be constantly forewarned by those who are suspicious.

Lack of Resolution

A timid woman should never marry a hesitating man, lest, like frightened children, each keeps perpetually re-alarming the other by imaginary fears; nor yet a careless man, for he would commit just

indiscretions enough to keep her in perpetual "fear and trembling"; but one should marry one who is bold, yet judicious, so that her intellect, by reposing in his tried judgment, can feel safe, and let her

JAMES RANDOLPH—SLIM NECK; LONG FACE; SHARP FEATURES; TYPE OF "OLD-FASHIONED CONSUMPTIVE"; UNFORTUNATE ORGANIZATION.

trust in him quiet her natural fearfulness.

A hopeless man should marry a resolute, hopeful woman, who is always telling how well things are going to turn out, and encouraging, and who has sufficient judgment to be allowed the reins, lest the fears of both render him pusillanimous, and their children cowards. Many men live tame lives, though abundantly capable of accomplishing almost anything, because too irresolute to once begin; whereas, with a judicious yet expectant wife to prompt them to take initiatory steps, they would fill responsible positions.

An industrious, thrifty, hard-

THEODORE THOMAS—MOTIVE TEMPERAMENT; WELL-BALANCED PHYSIQUE; WELL KNOWN MUSICAL DIRECTOR; ADAPTED TO ONE WHO IS SIMILARLY AN ENTHUSIAST IN MUSIC.

working man should marry a woman tolerably saving and industrious. As the "almighty dollar" is now the great motor-wheel of humanity, and that to which most husbands devote their entire lives, to delve alone is uphill work. Much more if she indulges in extravagance. It is doubly important, therefore, that both work together pecuniarily. But if either has property enough to create in both a

feeling of contentment, large acquisition in the other is less important; yet a difference here often engenders opposition elsewhere.

Good livers should marry—he to provide table luxuries, she to serve them up, and both to enjoy them together. Indeed, a good appetite in both can often be made to harmonize other discordant points, and promote concord.

The irritable, yet approbative, must by no means marry those like themselves, lest the irritability of each, by blaming the other, rouse mutual resentment. Yet if such are married, both must be especially careful how they cast any reflections; because the other party construes them to mean much more than was intended. Probably more conjugal animosities originate in this wounded ambition than in any other faculty. Nothing as effectually rouses and intensifies every existing antagonism. Pride is a good thing but must be respected and humored, at least not upbraided, or mortified. Even if a man can gratify a woman's love of style and display, he must not censure her in private unless he is willing to kindle her hate, and spoil their children.

Fault-finding beaux and girls during courtship, are sure to scold intolerably after marriage. If your moderate ambition can endure censure, marry; but if not, take timely warning from "straws." Once who is hard to please before marriage, will be much harder after; while one who patiently endures and forbears during courtship, will be more so after marriage, if kept in a love mood; and a beau who insists on having his way before, will be dogmatical if not domineering after; and must marry a meek, patient, accommodating woman.

This counterbalancing law also governs the intellectual faculties. If a man who has large perceptives with small reflectives, marries a woman having large reflectives with small perceptives, since both transmit what is strongest in themselves, their children will inherit his large perceptives along with her large reflectives; thus possessing the perfections of both, unmarred by the imperfections of either. He can remember, but not think; while she can think, but not remember; yet their children can both think and remember.

This is true of memory and judgment, of language and sense, of poetry and philosophy, of each and all the intellectual capacities, so that these offsettings can be made to improve tall marriages as well as offspring. When both have the safe defects their offspring will show these defects in a greater degree.

THE ETHICS & AESTHETICS OF EATING

LOUISE FISKE BRYSON, *EVERY DAY ETIQUETTE* (1893)

❧ ❧

*"God may forgive sins, but awkwardness has no forgiveness
in heaven or earth."—Hawthorne*

THE FIRST law of the table is to do nothing that might be unpleasant to others. At table more than elsewhere, all personal predilection, habit, and peculiarity must be kept in the background.

Too much stress cannot be laid on the importance of refinement at the table, both in manners and in the laying and service of the table itself. The habit of eating together and at stated times is one of the distinguishing marks that separate civilized men from savages, and a man's behavior at table is a pretty sure indication of his social standing.

"Eat at your own table as you would eat at the table of the king," said the wise Confucius. And he was right, for only by constant self-command in the matter of trifles can good habits at table be maintained.

A man may pass muster in dress and conversation, but if he is not perfectly familiar with the usages of good society, dinner will betray him.

Unpleasant peculiarities— abruptness, coarseness, noisiness—are especially offensive at table, for it is easier to be disgusted at that time than at any other.

To be prompt but not too early for dinner, is a rigid necessity. Five, ten, or fifteen minutes is the customary interval between arriving and the hour appointed. The Duke of Wellington's time was "five minutes before the time." To be late is a wrong to the hosts, to other guests, and to the dinner.

Replies to invitations to breakfasts, dinners, and formal teas should be sent immediately, so that vacancies may be filled. Delay is unpardonable. An empty chair at a feast is a depressing object—almost as bad as a skeleton.

To insure a well-ordered, well-appointed table, the mistress of the house must supervise it herself. Unless a thoroughly trained butler or waitress has charge of the dining-room, the wise housekeeper will wash the morning silver, glass, and china directly after breakfast, put

The flowers used should have a delicate and agreeable perfume, for strong odors destroy the aroma of daintily prepared dishes and banish one source of enjoyment.

The decorations of the table should be arranged high enough for the guests to see under them, or low enough for them to see over all flowers or ornaments.

the sideboard in order, wash dingy glass or silverware in hot suds, and keep the dining room up to the required standard of elegance. An early morning impetus of this kind is usually sufficient to secure from the maid careful attention to details for the rest of the day.

A wise mistress goes to the dining-room about five minutes before meals, to see that the table is well arranged and that all deficiencies are supplied before the family arrives.

Flowers are the most beautiful of table decorations.

Formal meals are announced by a servant, who says in a low tone, "Dinner is served," or "Luncheon is served." Ringing a bell is quite out of fashion as a formal summons.

Preference for white or dark meat, rare or well done, should be expressed at once, and all food taken or declined promptly in courteous terms.

It is an evidence of absence of mind, to state it mildly, to handle the glass, silver, china, or the food unnecessarily.

Bread should be broken and

not cut before it is buttered or eaten. Biscuits, muffins, and gems are also broken.

Butter is not a necessity at dinner, and its absence is no evidence of excessive economy. It is assumed that the dishes are properly seasoned, and therefore require no further additions.

Potato-skins, orange-peel, etc.,

from the side rather than the point of the fork.

Remember that it is the Anglo-Saxon who strenuously objects to putting the knife in the mouth. The knife-line does not exist in full force in all parts of the Continent, as Thackeray humorously chronicles in his accounts of the royal Pumpernickels.

do not belong on the table-cloth. Though it grieve us, they must be put upon the plate.

Do not raise the arms like wings when cutting food. Keep the elbows as close to the sides as free movement will allow.

Cut food slowly, and never attack it as though it were a wild beast that must be conquered with all possible haste. "Whoever is in a hurry," says Lord Chesterfield, "shows that the thing he is about is too big for him."

Take small mouthfuls, and dispose of them slowly, taking them

Do not drink when there is food in the mouth.

When a person chokes, a blow on the back will usually dislodge the irritating particle. The nearest neighbor may give the blow, just between the shoulders, and do a great kindness.

If a glass of water or a cup of tea or coffee is overturned, quietly pick up the offending object, and lay the table-napkin, folded double, over the damp spot. Leave the rest to the servant, who will probably come to the rescue.

Do not tip up a soup-plate. But

if the desire to do so is unconquerable, tip it from you, and turn the spoon from instead of toward you.

In removing vegetables from a vegetable-dish, put the side of the spoon under the vegetables, not the point, and lift them out laterally.

Cut up salad on the plate as you prefer it. Then discard the knife, and eat it with a fork.

Do not be so absent-minded as to use a napkin for a pocket handkerchief.

Be wary of the use of the handkerchief at table. If the operation is anything but the briefest, it is better to seek temporary seclusion.

Emulate in one particular the nun who knew not the French of Paris. "No morsel from her lippe fell," says Chaucer.

Let the children talk occasionally at table. How are they to learn to converse well if they never have any practice? At the same time, they must not monopolize conversation or attention. This is an injustice to all, to children and their elders, alike.

Fra Bonvincina da Riva treats of fifty courtesies in his "courtesy book," which should be observed at table. This is a specimen, and furnishes good advice for the present day. "Fifth courtesy: Sit properly at board, courteous, well dressed, cheerful, and obliging. Thou must not sit anxious, nor dismal, nor lolling, nor with thy legs crossed, nor awry, nor leaning forward."

Wine glasses and goblets are held by the stem, not by the bowl.

Help girls before boys at table, and very little children before anyone else.

Turn away the head when about to cough or sneeze, putting the handkerchief to the face—if there is time.

Be calm and unruffled when accidents happen. If a guest spills gravy, coffee, sauce, etc., it is better for him not to apologize, but to appear to be unaware of the misadventure. Ask the servant for a clean fork or spoon when that article has been dropped.

Use a fork for breaking up and eating potatoes.

Oil, vinegar, and mustard are set on the table in little ornamental bottles and jugs. Individual salt-cellars and butter-plates form a part of each cover.

Salt is taken from an individual salt-cellar with the knife, and shaken over the food by knocking the knife gently against the fingers of the left hand. From a large salt-cellar it is removed by means of a salt spoon, and deposited on the side of the plate.

Gentlemen stay at a table a short time after ladies have left it, discussing wines, cigars, and liqueurs (or cordials), and no doubt indulging in the most improving conversation.

Sherry, Madeira, and port are always decanted, and placed on the

sideboard ready for use. Claret is not usually decanted in America. It should never be iced, but should be about the temperature of the room. Champagne and sparkling wines are kept in an ice-pail until just before they are served. They are never decanted, but poured out as quickly as possible after opening.

Sherry is the proper wine to accompany soup. Chablis, hock, sauterne, go with fish; claret and champagne with the roast. Sherry and claret, or Burgundy, are again offered with the dessert, the after-dinner wines being of superior quality to those served during the meal. Cordials or liqueurs come after the dessert.

The aesthetic movement in this country is nowhere more visible than in the arrangement and appointments of the table. The tendency is toward greater elegance and refinement, and consequently toward greater simplicity.

The need of "a perfect self-containedness" at a dinner-table, where food and sentiments may not be to our liking, often makes itself felt. If wine is provided, and the guest does not approve of it, a private table is not a suitable place for expressing individual convictions. He may receive the wine in the different glasses sparingly and make no comment. If toasts are proposed, he will lift his glass and be courteous.

A request to dine, whether accepted or declined, necessitates a call upon the hostess within ten days, except when grief or illness has been mentioned as the cause of sending a regret.

Fine linen, napkins of generous size, attractive china and glassware, polished silver, and appropriate light, all aid in establishing and maintaining a proper standard of manners.

Remember that the law of proportion is the law of beauty, and that guests are sure to enjoy a comparatively modest entertainment suited to the means and habits of the household far more than something ambitious that has strained every nerve and left the host and hostess jaded and depressed.

A host must plan a dinner carefully beforehand, as a successful general plans a battle; but when the conflict begins, he must, like the latter, have courage and calmness. The hostess must smile, "though china fall" and every dish turn out a failure.

For a perfect feast, brilliant and agreeable conversation is as indispensable as a handsome and well-furnished table.

Glasses, knives, and oyster-forks are placed at the right of each plate; other forks are placed at the left, and also the napkin. A formal cover (that is, a plate and other necessities for each person) has two large knives, a small silver knife and fork for fish, three large forks, a tablespoon for soup, a small oyster-fork for eating raw oysters, and a goblet for water. Where wine is used, glasses for claret, hock, champagne, etc., are placed around the goblet.

Soup and fish are distinct courses.

Dishes which are served in the first course after fish are called *entrees*. Then comes the roast. Dishes following the roast are called *entremets*. Next in order is game, then salad (for game and salad), and last, the dessert, followed by black coffee.

Before the dessert is set on, everything is cleared from the table, except the decorations and lights, and the crumbs are removed with a silver crumb-scraper or a clean napkin and plate.

A servant should offer wine on the right hand, and all dishes on the left.

Do not imagine for an instant that because a man eats with his knife, or leans back in his chair, or reaches across the table to help himself, or takes up corn on the cob with both hands, that he is necessarily an ill-bred person. Good breeding is an affair of more than one thing, of more than four or of four hundred. It is a matter of self-respect and respect for others. A supercilious young woman paid a visit of a week to a distant city, and during that time noted forty mistakes made by her entertainers.

And not one of them could have been so gross an error as her reporting the fact!

Do not talk across the table at formal meals, nor speak across your next neighbors to those at a distance. Conversation should become general toward the close of a meal. Then each speaks as he has something to say.

Brillat-Savarin

Brillat-Savarin, the most intellectual of all dinner discoursing men, according to the author of *Social Etiquette of New York*, gives directions for an agreeable dinner-party, of which the following is the substance:

That conversation should be constantly general, the number of guests must not exceed twelve. Let the guests be chosen of various occupations, analogous tastes, and such points of contact that introductions are unnecessary.

Let the men have wit without pretension, and the women be pleasant without being coquettes.

Let the dishes be exceedingly choice, but *small in number*, and the wines of first quality, each in degree.

Let the order of serving be from the more substantial dishes to those that are lighter, and from the simpler wines to those of finer flavor.

Let everybody leave before eleven o'clock, and everybody in bed by twelve.

Ice in a glass of water or wine is hazardous, for it sometimes causes the unwary drinker to make a disagreeable sound.

When a meal is over, lay the knife and fork side by side across the plate, not directly pointing from the body, but a little crosswise, to prevent possible accidents from the handles catching in a loose sleeve or lace.

Don't eat fast, or gorge, says the gentle author of *Don't*. Always take plenty of time. Haste is vulgar. "Hurry was made for slaves."

Soup is eaten from the side of the spoon, and not from the end. Avoid gurgling and drawing in the breath and making noises when eating soup. Decline a second service of soup. It delays the dinner. Always accept the first service, whether desired or not, and appear to partake of it.

Vegetables are eaten with a fork, also cheese, croquettes, pat-ties, sometimes ice-cream and puddings that are not too soft. The rule is not to eat anything with a spoon that can be eaten with a fork.

Olives, Jerusalem artichokes, asparagus, and celery are eaten with the fingers.

Corn on the cob is taken in one hand. The ear should be broken once or twice before being raised to the mouth, thus enabling us to avoid too close a resemblance to our *congener* the pig.

Don't leave the knife and fork on the plate when it is sent for a second supply of food.

A guest should not fold up his napkin when leaving the table, but lay it down loosely beside the plate.

The spoon is not left in the tea or coffee cup. This habit is frequently the cause of upsetting the cup. Let the spoon lie in the saucer.

The spoon is used for water-ices, Roman punch, soup, puddings, tea and coffee, preserved and canned fruits, and for all berries; in fact for whatever is too liquid to be managed with a fork.

Pineapple requires a knife and fork. Bananas should be peeled and sliced with a knife, and eaten with a fork.

Dip the tips of the fingers in a finger-bowl after eating fruit or after dinner, pass the fingers thus moistened here and there across the mouth, then wipe both mouth and fingers delicately on the napkin—a fruit napkin, if one has been provided.

A monotonous dietary impeaches alike the intelligence and benevolence of the one who provides it. There are fashions in food that many follow from mere force of habit. Food can be infinitely varied, and yet remain simple and wholesome. Habits at table are better when there is the charm of variety in food and the pleasant surprise of new dishes.

Go to the table as if every meal were a feast, with quiet composure and a thankful heart, with something light and interesting to say, and the disposition to be pleased with everything.

Signal to Cranes

Naval Training Manual

⚹ ⚹

HOIST. With forearm vertical, forefinger pointing up,
move hand in small horizontal circle clockwise.

HOIST. Hold both arms
horizontal at sides, fully
extended, and move upward
and return.

LOWER. Hold arms at sides,
fully extended, and move
out and return.

RAISE BOOM. Arm extended,
fingers closed, thumb
pointing upward, move
hand up and down.

LOWER BOOM. ARM EXTENDED, FINGERS CLOSED, THUMB POINTING DOWN, MOVE HAND UP AND DOWN.

MOVE SLOWLY. USE ONE HAND TO GIVE THE HOIST, LOWER, RAISE BOOM, LOWER BOOM, SWING BOOM, TRAVEL, OR RACK, AND PLACE OTHER HAND MOTIONLESS NEAR THE HAND GIVING THE MOTION SIGNAL. (HOIST SLOWLY SHOWN AS EXAMPLE.)

LOWER BOOM AND RAISE LOAD. GIVE LOWER BOOM SIGNAL WITH ONE HAND AND RAISE LOAD SIGNAL WITH OTHER HAND.

TRAVEL. ARM EXTENDED FORWARD, HAND OPEN AND SLIGHTLY RAISED, WAVE FOREARM IN DIRECTION OF TRAVEL WHILE FACING IN THAT DIRECTION.

How to Lose at Checkers

COLLIER'S CYCLOPEDIA (1882)

❧ ❧

THE LOSING game of draughts is rarely understood, and therefore rarely appreciated. We believe that there is even more foresight required in the losing than in the winning game of draughts, for it is equally as necessary to see several moves on ahead, and the game may be almost instantly lost by a thoughtless move.

To win at the losing game we must compel our adversary to take all our men, and the novice usually commences by losing as many men as possible. This proceeding is an error; the player has the advantage who has the most men on the table, as will be instanced by one or two examples.

Suppose white to have a king on each of the four squares, 1, 2, 3, 4; black, one on 31. First, we will suppose that white commences thus:—

White	Black
4 to 8	31 to 27
3 to 7	27 to 23
2 to 6	23 to 18
1 to 5	

Black must now retreat, for, if he moves to 14 or 15, the game is lost, as he may be compelled to take each of his opponent's men in succession. Thus, suppose he move to 14:—

White	Black
5 to 9	14 to 5
6 to 9	5 to 14
7 to 10	14 to 7
8 to 11 and wins.	

Thus black's move must be a retreat in answer to white's 1 to 5. Then,

Black	White
18 to 22	5 to 9
22 to 26	6 to 14
26 to 31	14 to 18
31 to 27	

Black.

White.

At this point, if white advanced from 18 to 23 to be taken, he would lose the game unless very careful, as the lost man would have the move against him. His best move, therefore, would be 18 to 25. If black moves to 24, he loses. Black had better move to 32, and white 6 to 10.

Suppose white's men to be placed from 21 to 32. If then we can secure one of the adversary's men at 21, we are almost certain to lose all our men first, and thus to win the game, for, by keeping this man blocked until required, he can be made use of at the right time. Let us take an example, white moving first.

We will now point out the best "traps" for the losing game.

Black	White
32 to 28	8 to 11
28 to 32	15 to 19
32 to 28	19 to 24
28 to 19	10 to 15
19 to 3	11 to 7,
	and wins.

White	Black
22 to 18	9 to 14
22 to 18	5 to 14*
22 to 18	14 to 21
22 to 18	11 to 16
20 to 11	7 to 16
23 to 18**	10 to 15
18 to 11	8 to 15
28 to 24	15 to 00
24 to 15	6 to 10
15 to 6	1 to 10

· 55 ·

White	Black
26 to 22	4 to 8
27 to 23	16 to 19
23 to 16	12 to 19
22 to 18	10 to 15
18 to 4	3 to 8
4 to 11	2 to 7
11 to 2	

*Very bad play; this ought to have been 6 to 13.

**Not a good move, but will serve to illustrate the advantages of man at 21.

White now has six men on the board, whilst black has only two; but white can reduce this number at any time by moving 30 to 26. Black can only move 19 to 24 or to 23. Suppose he move it to 23, then it will be better for white to reduce black to one as follows:—

White	Black
31 to 27	23 to 26
30 to 23	21 to 30
29 to 25	30 to 21
32 to 28	21 to 17
28 to 24	17 to 14

If black move to 18, 10, or 9, he loses at once, so 14 to 17 is the best move. If white move 27 to 23 he loses the game, for black would move 17 to 22, from which white could not escape. Hence the game would be best played by

White	Black
2 to 6	17 to 21
6 to 10	21 to 25
10 to 14	25 to 30
14 to 17	

The game might now be prolonged, but still to win the losing game with the four against one is almost a certainty, as it can only be lost by an oversight.

Rubbing-Stick Fire

Ernest Thompson Seton (1903)

❧ ❧

I HAVE certainly made a thousand fires with rubbing sticks, and have made at least five hundred different experiments. So far as I can learn, my own record of thirty-one seconds from taking the sticks to having the fire ablaze is the world's record, and I can safely promise this: That everyone who will follow the instructions I now

thick, twelve to fifteen inches long; roughly rounded, sharpened at each end as in the cut.

Block or Board—Two inches wide, six or eight inches long, five-eighths of an inch thick. In this block, near one end, cut a side notch one-half an inch deep, wider on the under side; and near its end half an inch from the edge, make a

give will certainly succeed in making a rubbing-stick fire.

Take a piece of dry, sound, balsam-fir wood (or else cedar, cypress, tamarac, basswood, or cottonwood, in order of choice) and make of it a drill and a block, thus:

Drill—Five-eighths of an inch

little hollow or pit in the top of the block, as in the illustration.

Tinder—For tinder, use a wad of fine, soft, very dry, dead grass mixed with shredded cedar bark, birch bark, or even cedar wood scraped into a soft mass.

Bow—Make a bow of any bent

stick two feet long, with a strong buckskin or belt-lacing thong on it.

Socket—Finally you need a socket. This simple little thing is made in many different ways. Sometimes I use a pine or hemlock knot with a pit one-quarter inch deep, made by boring with the knife point. But it is a great help to have a good one made of a piece of smooth, hard stone or marble, set in wood; the stone or marble having in it a smooth round pit three-eighths inch wide and three-eighths inch deep. The one I use most was made by an Eskimo. A view of the underside is shown in cut I.

Now we are ready to make the fire.

Under the notch in the fire-block, set a thin chip.

Turn the leather thong of the bow once around the drill; the thong should now be quite tight. Put one point of the drill into the pit of the block, and on the upper end put the socket, which is held in the left hand, with the top of the drill in the hole of the stone. Hold the left wrist against the left shin, and the left foot on the fire-block. Now, draw the right hand back and forth steadily on level and the full length of the bow. This causes the drill to twirl in the pit. Soon it bores in, grinding out powder, which presently begins to smoke. When there is a great volume of smoke from the growing pile of black powder, you know that you have the spark. Cautiously lift the block, leaving the smoking powder on the chip. Fan this with your hand till the live coal appears. Now, put a wad of the tinder gently on the spark; raise the chip to a convenient height, and blow till it bursts into flame. N.B.—

(1) The notch must reach the middle of the firepit.

(2) You must hold the drill steadily upright, and cannot do so without bracing the left wrist against the left shin, and having the block on firm foundation.

(3) You must begin lightly and slowly, pressing heavily and sawing fast after there is smoke.

(4) If the fire does not come, it is because you have not followed these instructions.

The Art of Mind-Reading Revealed

George Beard, *Popular Science Monthly* (1888)

❧ ❧

IN THE history of science and notably in the history of physiology and medicine, it has often happened that the ignorant and obscure have stumbled upon facts and phenomena which, though wrongly interpreted by themselves, yet, when investigated and explained, have proved to be of the highest interest. The phenomena of the emotional trance, for example, had been known for ages, but not until Mesmer forced them on the scientific world, by his public exhibitions and his ill-founded theory of animal magnetism, did they receive any serious and intelligent study. Similarly the general fact that mind may so act on body as to produce involuntary and unconscious muscular motion was by no means unrecognized by physiologists, and yet not until the "mind-reading" excitement was it demonstrated that this principle could be utilized for the finding of any object or limited locality on which a subject, with whom an operator is in physical connection, concentrates his mind.

Although, as I have since ascertained, experiments of this kind have been previously performed in a quiet, limited way in private circles, and mostly by ladies, yet very few had heard of or witnesses them; they were associated in the popular mind very naturally with "mesmerism," or "animal magnetism," and by some were called "mesmeric flames." The physiological explanation had never been even suggested; hence the first public exhibitions of Brown, with his brilliantly successful demonstrations of his skill in this direction, were a new revelation to physiologists as well as to the scientific world in general.

The method of mind-reading,

introduced by Brown, which is but one of many methods that have been or may be used, is as follows:

The operator, usually blindfolded, firmly applies the back of the hand of the subject to be operated on against his own forehead, and with his other hand presses lightly upon the palm and fingers of the subject's hand. In this position he can detect, if sufficiently expert, the slightest movement, impulse, tremor, tension, or relaxation, in the arm of the subject. He then requests the subject to concentrate his mind on some locality in the room, or on some hidden object, or on some one of the letters of the alphabet suspended along the wall. The operator, blind-folded, marches sometimes very rapidly with the subject up and down the room or rooms, up and down stairways, or out-of-doors through the streets, and, when he comes near the locality on which the subject is concentrating his mind, a slight impulse, or movement is communicated to his hand by the hand of the subject.

This impulse is both involuntary and unconscious on the part of the subject. He is not aware, and is unwilling, at first, to believe, that he gives any such impulse; and yet it is sufficient to indicate to the expert and practiced operator that he has arrived near the hidden object, and then, by a close study and careful trials in different directions, upward, downward, and at various points of the compass, he ascertains precisely the locality, and is, in many cases, as confident as though he had received verbal communication from the subject.

Even though the article on which the subject concentrates his mind be very small, it can quite frequently be picked out from a large number, provided the subject be a good one, and the operator sufficiently skillful. The article is sometimes found at once, with scarcely any searching, the operator going to it directly, without hesitation, and with a celerity and precision that, at first sight, and until the physiological explanation is understood, justly astonished even the most thoughtful and skeptical. (In New Haven I saw Brown, before a large audience, march off rapidly through the aisle and find at once the person on whom the subject was concentrating his mind, although there was the privilege of selecting any one out of a thousand or more present.) These experiments, it should be added, are performed in public or private, and on subjects of unquestioned integrity, in the presence of experts, and under a combination of circumstances and conditions for the elimination of sources of error that make it necessary to rule out at once the possibility of collusion.

The alternative is, therefore, between the actual transfer of thought from subject to operator, as has been claimed, and the theory of unconscious muscular motion and relaxation on the part of the subject, the truth of which I have demonstrated by numerous experiments.

One of the gentlemen with whom I have experimented, Judge Blydenberg, who began to test his powers directly after I first called public attention to the subject in New Haven, claims to succeed, even with the most intellectual persons, provided they fully comply with the conditions, and honestly and persistently concentrate their minds. One fact of interest, with regard to his experiments, is the exceeding minuteness of the objects he finds. A large number of the audience empty their pockets

on the table, until it is covered with a medley of keys, knives, trinkets, and miscellaneous small objects. Out of them the subject selects a small seed a little larger than a pea, and even this the operator,

after some searching, hits precisely.

One may take a large bunch of keys, throw them on the table, and he picks out the very one on which the subject concentrates his mind.

Another fact of interest in his experiments is that, if a subject thinks over a number of articles in different parts of the room, and, after some doubt and hesitation, finally selects some one, the operator will lead him, sometimes successively, to the different objects on which he has thought, and will wind up with the one that he finally selected. He also performs what is known as the "double test," which consists in taking the hand of a third party, who knows nothing of the hidden object, but who is connected with another party who does know, and who concentrates his mind upon it. The connection of these two persons is made at the wrist, and the motion is communicated from one to the other through the arms and hands. The "double test" has been regarded by some as an argument against the theory that this form of mind-reading was simply the utilizing of unconscious muscular motion on the part of the persons operated upon.

This gentleman represents that the sensation of muscular thrill is very slight indeed, even with good subjects; and, in order to detect it, he directs his own mind as closely as possible to the hand of the subject.

In all these experiments, with all mind-readers, the requirement for the subject to concentrate the mind on the locality agreed upon is absolute; if that condition is not fulfilled, nothing can be done, for the very excellent reason that, without such mental concentration, there will be no unconscious muscular tension or relaxation to guide the operator.

Experiments of the following kind I have made repeatedly with the above-named gentlemen:

A dozen or more pins may be stuck about one inch or an inch apart into the edge of a table; I concentrate my mind on any one of these pins, telling no one. The operator enters the room, gets the general direction of the object in the usual way, and, when he has come near to the row of pins, he will limit the physical connection to one of his index-fingers, pressing firmly against one of mine, and in this way he soon finds the head of the pin on which my mind has been concentrated. The only limitation of area in the locality that can be found by a good mind-reader with a good subject is that two objects should not be so near to each other that the finger of the operator strikes on both at once.

J. Stanley Grimes thus describes the performance of a mind-reader in Chicago: "I repeatedly witnessed similar performances with different experts in this branch and under circumstances where every element of error from intentional or unintentional collusion was rigidly excluded. At the request of the company the same young lady was again sent from the room and blindfolded, as on previous occasions. The gentleman requested the company to suggest anything they desired the subject should be willed to do, thus removing any possibility of a secret agreement to deceive between the parties. It was suggested that the young lady should be brought into the room and placed in a position with her face toward the north; that the gentleman should then place his fingers upon her shoulder as before; that she should turn immediately to the right facing the south and proceed to a certain figure in the parlor-carpet; then turning to the west, she was to approach a sofa in a remote corner of the room, from which she should remove a small tidy, which she should take to the opposite side of the room, and place it upon the head of a certain young gentleman in the company; she was then to proceed to the extreme end of the parlor, and take a coin from the right vest pocket of a gentleman, and return to the opposite side of the room, and place the coin in the left vest pocket of another gentleman named; she was then to remove the tidy from the head of the gentleman upon whom it had been

placed, and return it to the tête-à-tête where she originally found it.

"I must confess to no little surprise when I saw the young lady perform with the most perfect precision every minute detail as above described, and with the most surprising alacrity; in fact so quick were her motions that it was with the greatest difficulty that the gentleman could keep pace with the young lady's movements."

In order to settle the question beyond dispute whether unconscious muscular action was the sole cause of this success in finding objects, I made the following crucial experiments with this lady: Ten letters of the alphabet were placed on a piano, the letters being written on large pieces of paper. I directed her to see how many times she would get a letter which was in the mind of one of the observers in the room correctly by chance purely, without any physical touch. She tried ten times and got it right twice. I then had her try ten experiments with the hand of the person operated on against the forehead of the operator, the hand of the operator lightly touching against the fingers of this hand, and the person operated on concentrating her mind all the while on the object, and looking at it. In ten experiments tried this day, with the same letters, she was successful six times. I then tried the same number of experiments with a wire, one end being attached to the head or hand of the subject, and the other end to the head or hand of the operator. The wire was about ten feet long and was so arranged—being made fast at the middle to a chair—that no unconscious muscular motion could be communicated through it from the person on whom she was operating. She was successful but once out of ten times. Thus we see that by pure chance she was successful twice out of ten times; by utilizing unconscious muscular action in the method of Brown she was successful six times out of ten. When connected by a wire she was less successful than when she depended on pure chance without any physical connection. In order still further to confirm this, I suggested to this lady to find objects with two persons touching her body in the manner we have above described. I told these two to deceive her, concentrating their minds on the object hidden, at the same time using conscious motion toward some other part of the room. These experiments several times repeated, showed that it was possible to deceive her, just as we found it possible to deceive other muscle-readers.

The question of whether it is possible for one to be a good muscle-reader and pretty uniformly successful, and yet not know just how the trick is done, must be answered in the affirmative. It is possible to become quite an adept in this art without suspecting even remotely the physiological explanation. The muscular tension necessary to guide the operator is but slight, and the sensation it produces may be very easily referred by credulous, uninformed operators to the passage of "magnetism;" and I am sure that with a number of operators on whom I have experimented this mistake is made. Some operators declare that they cannot tell how they find the locality, that their success is to them a mystery; these declarations are made by private, amateur performers, who have no motive to deceive me, and whose whole conduct during the experiments confirms their statements. Other operators speak of thrills or vibrations which they feel, auras and all sorts of indefinable sensations. These manifold symptoms are purely subjective, the result of mind acting on the body, the emotions of wonder and expectancy developing various phenomena that are attributed to "animal magnetism," "mesmerism" or "electricity"—in short, to everything but the real cause. I have seen amateurs who declared that they experienced these sensations when trying without success to read mind through the wires, or perhaps without any connection with the subject whatever. Persons who are in the vicinity of galvanic batteries, even though not in the circuit, very often report similar experiences.

PHOTO-SCULPTURE

CHAMBER'S ENCYCLOPEDIA (1868)

❧ ❧

PHOTO-SCULPTURE, a new art, invented, during the present year [1868] by M. Willeme, a Frenchman. It has been introduced into Great Britain, and is successfully practiced by Mr. Claudet in London, and a society has been formed for carrying it out in Paris. It consists in taking likenesses in the form of statuettes and medallions by the aid of photography, and a very ingenious series of accessory contrivances. A building specially adapted for the purpose is absolutely necessary; this consists of a circular room, 40 feet in diameter, and surmounted by a glass cupola 22 feet high, the supporting wall being about 8 feet in height, and pierced with 24 equidistant holes about 4 feet from the floor; these are only sufficiently large to permit the action of an ordinary camera lens through each one. Outside the surrounding wall of

this circular chamber is a covered dark passage, in which twenty-four cameras are placed with their lenses adjusted to the holes in the wall. The person whose likeness is to be taken stands in the center under the glass dome, and at a given signal the cameras are simul-

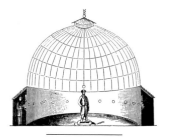

FIGURE 1

taneously brought into action, and a photograph is taken. The whole of this arrangement will be fully understood by reference to fig. 1.

The twenty-four photographs are carefully numbered, so that no error can take place in the subsequent operation, which is performed in another chamber: any room which can be darkened will do. It consists in placing them in consecutive order on a vertical wheel, which is so arranged that at the will of the operator each one can be brought before the lens of a magic lantern, and its image projected on a transparent screen, as in fig. 2. The modeling clay is so placed, rather behind the screen, that the artist can use a pantograph, which has its reducing point armed with a molding or cutting tool instead of a mere marker; and as the longer arm of the instrument describes the outline of the projected figures obtained from the photographs, the shorter one is reproducing on a smaller scale the figure in the clay. The statuette thus produced re-

FIGURE 2

quires retouching with the hand to remove the sharp and rugged lines of the cutting-tools, and of course much depends upon artistic skill in doing this. In the skilled hands which have yet had to do with its operations, the arrangement has had so marked a success as to promise to produce in time the most satisfactory results.

THE DANGERS OF TIGHT-LACING

W. BEACH, M. D., *AMERICAN PRACTICE OF MEDICINE* (1848)

❧ ❧

OF ALL the whims of fashion, no one is more absurd, or more mischievous in its effects, than that which condemns the female, under the pretence of improving the grace and beauty of her shape, to the torture of a tightly laced corset. Equally detrimental to comfort and to health, this portion of female attire cannot be too severely censured. It is productive of not the least advantage, real or imaginary, to compensate for the injury it produces, nor to excuse the folly of females in persisting in its use. The immediate effect of tight-lacing is, by compressing firmly the chest, to prevent its free expansion in the act of breathing; a less amount of air is taken into the lungs, and as a consequence, the blood is less perfectly changed. The impediment to breathing is increased when the corsets extend so low as to compress the abdomen; by the bowels being then forced upwards against the diaphragm (or partition between the chest and abdomen), the latter is prevented from descending, and the dimensions of the chest are thus contracted from below. A sense of oppression and weight is always experienced about the breast when the corset is drawn very tight; the breathing is short, quick, and panting; and not only is the blood prevented, from undergoing that change in the lungs by which it is

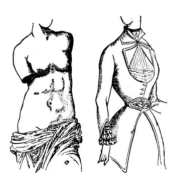

adapted for the healthy nourishment of the various organs, but the actions of the heart are also impeded; violent palpitation is not infrequently produced, accompanied with a sense of giddiness and occasional fainting. When the corset is worn constantly from early youth, the growth of the ribs is prevented, and the whole capacity of the chest is permanently contracted; and hence spitting of blood, difficulty of breathing, or even more dangerous and fatal diseases of the lungs and heart are induced. But it is not merely to the chest that the injurious effects of the corset are confined; it likewise compresses the whole of the upper portion of the abdomen (or bowels), and by the yielding nature of this portion of the body, the pressure upon the organs within is even more consid-

erable than that experienced by the heart and lungs. The liver, the stomach, and the bowels in particular, experience this pressure to a very great extent; in consequence, the free and healthy secretions of the liver are prevented from taking place, the stomach and the bowels can no longer perform their correct functions with proper vigor and regularity; the digestion of the food is impeded, and the bowels become costive and distended with wind. In this manner, in connection with the injury inflicted upon the lungs, the vigor of the whole system becomes prostrated, the skin assumes a sallow hue, the countenance a haggard, wrinkled appearance, and all the functions of life are performed imperfectly. It is a fact, that nothing is better adapted to produce the premature decay

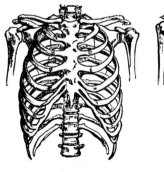
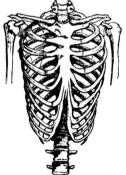

of beauty, and the early appearance of old age, than tight-lacing.

There are two other effects produced by this article of dress, which would be sufficient of themselves to induce every prudent and sensible female to abandon it. The first is the great injury inflicted upon the breasts, by which their proper development is prevented, and the nipple is almost entirely obliterated, so that, when called upon to fulfill the sacred office of nurse towards her offspring, the mother finds, to her sorrow, that, from her folly, she has totally incapacitated herself from performing its duties, or experiencing its pleasures. The second effect is that produced by the pressure of the corset upon the pelvis (hips) and the womb, more especially when worn in early youth, or during the first stages of pregnancy. From this cause barrenness, miscarriages, or a stunted and deformed offspring may result, or the pains, the difficulties, and the dangers of child-birth, may be increased to a frightful degree. Let no American woman talk about the Chinese women compressing their feet to prevent them from growing, so long as she continues the life-destroying custom of tight-lacing.

HOW TO MAKE SOUR KRAUT

REPORT OF THE DEPARTMENT OF AGRICULTURE (1869)

❧ ❧

A LETTER to the secretary upon the manufacture of sour kraut gives the following as the popular method of preparation among the kraut-makers of Lincoln County, Maine.

The outside and loose cabbage leaves should be cut off and the heads quartered and thrown into a tub of clear water, from which they should be taken, one piece or more at a time, and placed in a small box, open at top and bottom, and running in the grooves of the kraut machine, which is about four feet long, one foot wide, and six inches deep. The box runs over three or four knives, sometimes made of old scythes, fixed diagonally across the bottom of the machine. The edges of the knives are slightly raised above the level of the bottom, and when the box is moved backward and forward in the grooves, and pressure made with a small piece of

FILDERKRAUT

board on the cabbage, the latter is cut into thin, small slices, which drop in the tub beneath the cutter. As the cabbage is cut, it is transferred to a clean barrel (a pork barrel is preferable) and pounded with a heavy wooden mallet. The more closely it is packed the better; and, with care, from 250 to 300 pounds of cabbage may be put into a barrel of 40 gallons. One pint of fine salt to the barrel is sprinkled with the cabbage as it is packed down. No addition of water is required. Fill the barrel to a point two inches from the top, cover the kraut with large cabbage leaves, and place over the whole a wooden cover small can be made in two hours by two men. Any prejudice existing against sour kraut, for want of

CURLED SAVOY

NEWARK EARLY FLAT DUTCH

enough to be inserted within the barrel, where it must be kept firmly, by a heavy stone, until the process of fermentation is past. Place the barrel within five or six feet of the kitchen fire, and in a few days fermentation will commence, which may be hastened by the addition of a little blood-warm water; a frothy scum will rise and run off, when the kraut is all right and ready for use, and the barrel may be set in the cellar, porch, or shed. Freezing does it no injury, and it will keep in the cellar until March or April without depreciating, and longer in a cooler place. A barrel of kraut cleanliness, is not well founded where even ordinary care is exercised in its preparation. There are various modes of cooking it, while some prefer it raw, eating it as a salad. It is frequently boiled, three hours or more, with salt pork cut into small pieces. Perhaps the nicest style is to fry it in pork fat or with the gravy from roast pork. For frying, it should be boiled two hours to make it tender. It is a wholesome, hearty food, and is particularly appreciated by men requiring a substantial diet, while it is also relished by many of more fastidious taste.

HORSEBACK ETIQUETTE

TYLER M. KLICKMAN, *HOW TO BEHAVE CORRECTLY* (1898)

❧ ❦

KNOWING, as we do, the great aversion of American young ladies to out-door exercises, the following remarks may to them seem inappropriate; for the American girl is far behind her English cousin in the matter of a ten- or twenty-mile trot before breakfast, the early morning hours being the most popular for such exercise in England. Yet riding on horseback, which is the daily custom of English ladies, is rapidly becoming a fashionable amusement in this country; and riding clubs now exist in all large towns, the members of which are young ladies and gentlemen, who accompany each other on rides about the outskirts of the city. In this country the evening is the time usually selected for a fashionable ride through the thoroughfares of the city.

The ladies of England learned to ride during the reign of Charles II, when the queen, accompanied by ladies of the court and nobles in gay attire, rode forth with the king, and all were mounted on superb horses richly caparisoned. Of the ladies' riding habits Pepys says in his diary: "These riding habits are coats and doublets with deep skirts, just for all the world like mine, and doublets buttoned up the breast, and periwigs and hats, so that only for a petticoat dragging under their men's coats, nobody could take them for women in any point whatever."

The origin of the side-saddle, says an authority in such matters, is somewhat obscure. Early illuminated manuscripts show ladies riding sideways, and authorities attribute their introduction to Catherine de Medici. We know that pillions for ladies were used in the middle ages, a man being seated in front of the lady to guide the movements of the horse; and the Pilgrim fathers were wont to use the same style of seat for their wives in the early days of their settlement on New England shores. From this to the saddle with an arm was an easy transit, until progression evolved the side-saddle now in use.

The present style of riding habit is the short or medium length skirt, cloth drawers and short basque, with postilions and military collar, and a half-high silk hat with long veil floating, or the more becoming Derby hat with or without a plume. The simplest form of dress is the most elegant, but the habit should be made by a tailor, and fit perfectly but not too tight.

The elegance of a woman on horseback depends entirely on the flexibility of her figure. No woman can ride well enough to be worth looking at unless she is contented with a corset that will support the body without compressing the vital organs. A lady who intends to ride well can neither afford to cramp her muscles nor to impede the free circulation of her blood.

A stylist habit of invisible green, claret colored, or black cloth, or velvet with a jockey cap with visor to match, narrow linen collars and cuffs, gauntlet gloves of undressed kid of ivory tint, a jeweled or gold-mounted ivory-handled whip and a firm seat, and you have all the equipments for a ride in Rotten Row, or the Bois de Boulogne, or the Bloomington Road.

Ladies usually learn to ride at the riding academy, or with their fathers and brothers, before venturing out as riders with a party of equestrians. It is no compliment to the rest of the party to accept such an invitation unless you can ride well. Riding can not be acquired in a few lessons. The way in which to mount a horse, how to hold the reins and adjust the stirrup, can be easily learned, but it takes practice to become a fearless rider, to know how to sit properly, ride gracefully and make long distances without fatigue, to change your horse's gait at a moment's notice, and include your escort, the company, the landscape, and your route in your divided attention, but with a perfect comprehension.

A lady must never cling to her saddle or hang on the reins, or appear conscious of being in a novel

To swell the throng from every quarter

or uneasy situation. She should sit erect, but not lean back too far, nor incline to one side more than the other. By adjusting herself in exact momentum she will find herself mistress of her horse and her seat.

There is no accomplishment among the habits of exercise that is so becoming to a woman of fine presence as that of riding on horseback. It displays her figure to the finest advantage, her eyes sparkle, and her cheeks flush with the exhilarating motion, and her whole appearance is poetic and inspiring.

It is almost unnecessary to give any hints in regard to a gentleman's riding, as he is supposed to be trained to the saddle; but he may not know that etiquette demands that he shall always ride on a lady's right, never permit his horse to pass hers, and be quick to respond to her need of assistance. His horse should match hers, as nearly as possible, in size and pace, and he should ride the gait preferred by the lady with him.

The canter is the pace which ladies in this country prefer, because of its easy, rocking motion, and the slight knowledge of horsemanship it needs to acquire it. Adepts believe they have mastered the science of riding when they have reached this stage, but it is the simplest part. Trotting in an easy, regular gait, is much more difficult to learn, but a far better style. English women all ride trotting horses with the same facility with which the American woman lopes or canters.

To learn all the steps, changing from a canter to a trot, or a walk to a canter, requires considerable practice. Horses are trained to know, by a movement of the bridle hand, or a touch of the whip, which leg to lead off with, and whether they are desired to trot, gallop, or canter.

An old picture of Martha Washington on horseback shows her dressed in a princess habit, buttoned from the throat to the hem, narrow, full ruffles at the throat and wrists, tight coat sleeves, and a rose-bud with leaves at the throat. In her hand is her high hat, with long, floating veil. The painter has caught the exact pose of the figure, and his illustration is graceful and life-like.

A gentleman should dress in a jaunty and picturesque manner for riding. He may wear an ordinary dark suit, but his gloves should be gauntlets, and his hat a high silk one, or a military felt. His riding whip should be a heavy one with a carved handle, and his general appearance should be that of a cavalier, equipped with taste and elegance.

In riding, the reins are held lightly in the left hand, the whip in the right. The horn, or pommel, of the saddle must not be touched. The rider must learn to balance gracefully, and maintain the center of gravity by self-poise. A good rider equalizes her movements with those of her horse, and does not jolt up and down when changing her horse's pace.

Ladies who are assisted to mount a horse by a gentleman escort, place one hand on the saddle, the other on the gentleman's shoulder, as he kneels for the purpose, with the left foot in his hand, and, by a slight spring, are nicely seated in the saddle. The foot is then adjusted to the stirrup, and the habit neatly folded. Care should be taken to have the hair secure, as the motion of the horse may cause it to come down; the hat well fastened on, and the skirt of the habit well

buttoned at the waist. The exercise of riding is so violent, that it frequently seriously disarranges the toilet.

A lady who is invited to drive with a gentleman can not offer to take a friend with her, or, in case of sudden indisposition, substitute her friend for herself. She should never call upon friends and leave the gentleman to pass the time alone in the carriage, since it is presumable he invited her for the pleasure of her company.

Above all, she should avoid late hours if driving on a Summer evening. It devolves upon her to remind her escort that it is growing late. It may be a lovely moonlight night, and the temptation to prolong the drive may be very strong; but prudence suggests nine o'clock as the latest hour a careful young

lady would choose, unless there is a party driving in company, or the escort is an old and trusted friend or a relative. A true gentleman, who is careful that no word or act of his shall cause a moment's criticism, will never ask a young lady to compromise herself by driving with him at an unseemly hour. From seven to nine is long enough for a sociable and pleasant drive.

Fast driving should only be practiced with a fast horse, that can go without an effort. The absurdly frantic attempts of young gentlemen, to get a phenomenal amount of speed out of an ordinary animal, are both amusing and annoying. A pleasant, rapid trot is a much more enjoyable mode of driving than the break-neck speed which some young people indulge in. It is more respectable, as well as more elegant, to drive moderately, so that the horse shall become a secondary object, and the scenery and conversation form the principal features of interest.

Gentlemen may jump out of a carriage, but ladies should step out, taking time to bear their full weight on the step. Nothing is more ungainly than the habit—which went out with the high carriages—some gentlemen have of seizing a lady around the waist and bouncing her to the pavement. If the lady is obliged to alight with such assistance, let her place one hand on the shoulder of her escort, who will partially support her, as she steps down.

A gentleman should never drive with a lady without wearing gloves. It is customary for the gentleman driving to sit on the right of the lady, but some prefer the left side. In Boston, a gentleman always takes the left side, unless the lady is his wife, sister, or some near relative, so that it is easy to determine what relation his guest bears to him.

A lady should always feel certain of two things: that she has a safe escort and a safe horse. Then she can abandon herself to the enjoying of the drive with a sense of security and rest.

Lovers would do well to remember that hedges have ears as well as stone walls. Very absurd scenes of love-making have been witnessed and made merry over by hedgers and ditchers. An amusing story is told of a couple who became so absorbed in a tender conversation, that they drove into the open door of a wayside farmhouse, and surprised the family at supper. Love, however, does not seem to notice incongruities of situation, and is ready at all times, and in all places, to send out his mischievous arrows.

An eloping couple who were driving at full speed along the high-way were pursued by the girl's father on horseback, who, as he rode, shouted at the top of his voice: "Whoa, Kate! Whoa, Kate!" The runaways were stopped, and an effort made to return the girl to her father; but the old-gentleman said, coolly, "It's the hoss I want; you may keep the gal."

Driving

In England, when ladies and gentlemen go out in a carriage, they speak of the excursion as a drive, and use the term driving; and when they go out to ride, it is on a horse, and not in a carriage. The distinction has the sanction of custom; and it is correct to say, "I am going out to drive," even though you may not hold the reins. To say, "I am going riding," or, as some express it, "buggy riding," is vulgar.

A gentleman who accompanies ladies on a drive will remember, if the carriage is full, to sit with his back to the horses; he will know where to put his feet so as not to disarrange the ladies' dresses, and he will know when it is most convenient for the ladies to alight first, he handing them out, instead of stepping over them, to reach the pavement, and assist them out. When there is a footman as well as a coachman, gentlemen can, with propriety, be the last to leave the carriage; and it is the coachman's duty to open the carriage door and assist the ladies if they need any help. The greatest politeness in such matters is to do that which the least embarrasses the ladies.

A gentleman who acts as driver

ASSISTING THE LADY WHEN ALIGHTING FROM THE CARRIAGE.

must never allow himself to assist a lady into the carriage while he retains his seat. He must always alight and, holding the reins with one hand, assist the lady into the carriage with the other. He must be particular to see that the lap-robe is nicely arranged, and the lady's dress covered and protected from the wheel; and, if he stops for his companion to call on a friend, or at a store, he must alight each time to assist her out and in, waiting on the pavement during her stay.

Carriage Etiquette

Turning back to look at objects that have been passed; staring about and pointing to houses, or other parties in carriages, is rude. Laughing, or talking in a boisterous manner, or calling to persons on the sidewalk, is in very bad taste. People should not recline too much when driving, but maintain a dignified composure of manner, neither lolling on the seats, nor sitting bolt upright.

In England the driver turns to the left to pass another carriage. In this country he always turns to the right. It is never excusable to drive, in a violent manner, past another carriage going the same way. A slight slacking of ordinary speed in passing, especially if ladies are in the carriage, indicates proper training in the coachman and good breeding in the gentleman.

Young ladies who drive with a gentleman should resent the least approach to familiarity, such as insinuating an arm along the back of the seat, inclining the head as if in confidential conversation, and a free-and-easy air of ownership. Even when parties are engaged, such conduct looks very silly to other persons, and should be omitted as a most unsuitable display for the promenade or public thoroughfare.

If ladies accompanied by a gentleman stop to speak to ladies on the sidewalk, it is only courteous for the gentleman to step out and wait, with his hand on the door of the carriage, until the ladies are ready to drive on.

No gentleman will ever smoke when riding or driving with ladies.

Ladies who are invited to ride or drive with gentlemen, at a certain hour, should be ready exactly at the moment. It is neither well-bred nor dignified to keep any one waiting who has made an appointment conducive to your pleasure. Always make a careful toilet, looking bright and interested, with fresh gloves and ribbons, and a corsage knot of flowers. Have every thing ready, gloves on and buttoned, and all arrangements of the toilet complete, but do not seem to be in an eager state of expectancy.

METHOD OF RESTORING
THE APPARENTLY DEAD

RECOMMENDED BY THE ROYAL HUMANE SOCIETY (1879)

❧ ❧

From Intense Cold

RUB THE BODY with snow, ice, or cold water. Restore warmth by slow degrees. It is highly dangerous to apply heat too early.

From Drowning

Rule 1.—To adjust the Patient's Position.—Place the Patient on his back on a flat surface, inclined a little from the feet upwards; raise and support the head and shoulders on a small firm cushion or folded article of dress placed under the shoulder blades. Remove all tight clothing about the neck and chest.

Rule 2.—To maintain a Free Entrance of Air into the Windpipe.—Cleanse the mouth and nostrils; open the mouth; draw forward the Patient's tongue, and keep it forward; an elastic band over the tongue and under the chin will answer this purpose.

Rule 3.—To imitate the Movements of Breathing. First.—Induce Inspiration.—Place yourself at the

SYLVESTER'S METHOD—FIGURE 1

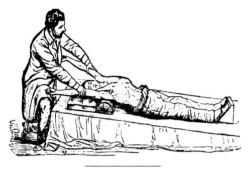

I.—INSPIRATION

head of the Patient, grasp his arms, raise them upwards by the sides of his head, stretch them steadily but gently upwards, for two seconds. (By this means fresh air is drawn into the lungs by raising the Ribs.)

Secondly.—Induce Expiration.—Immediately turn down the Patient's arms, and press them firmly but gently downwards against the sides of his chest, for two seconds. (By this means foul air is expelled from the lungs by depressing the Ribs.)

Thirdly.—Continue These Movements.—Repeat these measures alternately, deliberately, and perseveringly, fifteen times in a minute, until a spontaneous effort to respire be perceived. (By these means an exchange of air is produced in the lungs similar to that effected by natural respiration.)

When a spontaneous effort to respire is perceived, cease to Imitate the Movements of Breathing, and proceed to Induce Circulation and Warmth (as below).

Rule 4—To Excite Respiration.—During the employment of the above method excite the nostrils with snuff or smelling salts, or tickle the throat with a feather. Rub the chest and face briskly, and dash cold and hot water alternately on them. Friction of the limbs and body with dry flannel or cloths should be had recourse to. When there is a proof of returning respiration, the individual may be placed in a warm bath, the movements of the arms above described being continued until respiration is fully restored. Raise the body in twenty seconds to a sitting, position, dash cold water against the

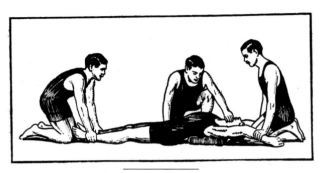

SYLVESTER'S METHOD—FIGURE 2

chest and face, and pass ammonia under the nose. Should a galvanic apparatus be at hand, apply the sponges to the region of diaphragm and heart.

Appearances Which Generally Indicate Death

There is no breathing nor heart's action; the eyelids are generally half-closed; the pupils dilated; the jaws clenched; the fingers semi-contracted; the tongue appearing between the teeth, and the mouth and nostrils are covered with a frothy mucus. Coldness and pallor of surface increases.

The treatment recommended by the Society is to be persevered in for three or four hours. It is an erroneous opinion that persons are irrecoverable because life does not soon make its appearance; as cases have come under the notice of the Society of a successful result even after five hours' perseverance—and it is absurd to suppose that a body must not be meddled with or removed without the permission of a Coroner.

Treatment after Natural Breathing Has Been Restored

To induce Circulation and Warmth.—Wrap the Patient in dry blankets, and rub the limbs upwards energetically. Promote the warmth of the body by hot flannels, bottles, or bladders of hot water, heated bricks, to the pit of the stomach, the armpits, and to the soles of the feet.

On the restoration of life, when the power of swallowing has returned, a teaspoonful of warm water, small quantities of wine, warm brandy and water, or coffee should be given. The Patient should be kept in bed, and a disposition to sleep encouraged. During reaction large mustard plasters to the chest and below the shoulders will greatly relieve the distressed breathing.

Note.—In all cases of prolonged immersion in cold water, when the breathing continues, a warm bath should be employed to restore the temperature.

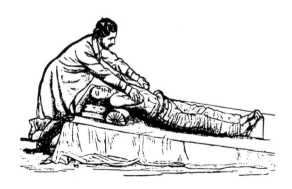

How to Climb a Ladder

United States Department of Agriculture Booklet

❧ ❧

B RACE lower end of ladder against base so it cannot slide, then grasp rung at upper end, using both hands.

Rise top end and walk forward under the ladder as shown, moving hands to grasp other rungs as you proceed.

When erect, lean ladder forward to position desired. Check angle, height, and stability at top and bottom.

All supporting points of stepladder should be level. Brace uneven points as shown.

When ground is soft or footing is uneven under one side of extension ladder, brace as shown.

Grip ladder firmly in climbing or descending. Wrap leg around rung when you are working.

Be sure shoes and rungs are free of mud or grass. Place feet squarely on rungs.

1) BRACE LOWER END OF LADDER AGAINST BASE SO IT CANNOT SLIDE, THEN GRASP RUNG AT UPPER END, USING BOTH HANDS. 2) RISE TOP END AND WALK FORWARD UNDER THE LADDER AS SHOWN, MOVING HANDS TO GRASP OTHER RUNGS AS YOU PROCEED. 3) WHEN ERECT, LEAN LADDER FORWARD TO POSITION DESIRED. CHECK ANGLE, HEIGHT, AND STABILITY AT TOP AND BOTTOM. 4) ALL SUPPORTING POINTS OF STEPLADDER SHOULD BE LEVEL. BRACE UNEVEN POINTS AS SHOWN.

1) WHEN GROUND IS SOFT OR FOOTING IS UNEVEN UNDER ONE SIDE OF EXTENSION LADDER, BRACE AS SHOWN. 2) GRIP LADDER FIRMLY IN CLIMBING OR DESCENDING. WRAP LEG AROUND RUNG WHEN YOU ARE WORKING. 3) BE SURE SHOES AND RUNGS ARE FREE OF MUD OR GRASS. PLACE FEET SQUARELY ON RUNGS. 4) TOP OF LADDER SHOULD EXTEND ABOVE THE EDGE OF ROOF BY AT LEAST THREE FEET.

1) THIS IS PROPER ANGLE FOR LADDER. DISTANCE OF LADDER FROM BUILDING AT BASE SHOULD BE ONE-FOURTH WORKING LENGTH OF LADDER. 2) SET LADDER WHERE WORK CAN BE REACHED WITH EASE. NEVER LEAN OUT TOO FAR TO ONE SIDE. 3) WITH LADDER OF PROPER LENGTH, USER CAN ALWAYS WORK MORE SAFELY AND CONVENIENTLY. 4) TOP OF STEPLADDER IS NOT MEANT FOR STANDING. THERE IS ALWAYS DANGER OF LOSING ONE'S BALANCE.

1) LADDER AS SHOWN IS PLACED AT TOO GREAT AN ANGLE, SUBJECTING IT TO STRAIN THAT CAN CAUSE IT TO BREAK OR SLIP. 2) UNCOMFORTABLE WORKING, AND WEIGHT OF USER IS UNEVENLY DISTRIBUTED, CAUSING OVERLOAD. 3) LADDER IS APT TO TIP BACKWARD OR FALL TO EITHER SIDE. BASE MUST NOT BE TOO NEAR OR TOO FAR FROM THE BUILDING. 4) WHEN LADDER IS TOO SHORT, IT IS UNSAFE AND DIFFICULT TO GET ONTO ROOF AND BACK AGAIN.

Top of ladder should extend above the edge of roof by at least three feet.

This is the proper angle for the ladder. Distance of ladder from building at base should be one-fourth working length of ladder.

Set ladder where work can be reached with ease. Never lean out too far to one side.

With ladder of proper length, user can always work more safely and conveniently.

Top of stepladder is not meant for standing. There is always danger of losing one's balance.

Ladder as shown is placed at too great an angle, subjecting it to strain that can cause it to break or slip.

Uncomfortable workings, and weight of user is unevenly distributed, causing overload.

Ladder is apt to tip backward or fall to either side. Base must not be too near or too far from the building.

When ladder is too short, it is unsafe and difficult to get onto roof and back again.

Sniggling for Eels

DANIEL C. BEARD, *BOY'S BOOK OF SPORTS* (1886)

❧ ❧

To sniggle for Eels, procure a strong top rod, or a long slender hazel stick, slip a small quill over the taper end, leaving the extreme end of the quill whole; a tailors button needle, off a stocking needle not more than two inches long, is also requisite, and a length of hard-twisted twine or fine whipcord for the line: tie the needle to the line with waxed silk, first laying the end of the line nearly half-way down the needle, the line will then hang from about the middle, leaving the smaller end bare. To bait the needle, enter the thick end of it into a well-scoured lob-worm near the tail, and carry it up to the head, so that the point of the needle may come out at the middle of the worm; then put the point of the needle into the end of the quill, and take the rod in one hand and the line in the other, when you may guide the bait into any of the well-known haunts of the Eel, viz. under large stones, into the holes of banks which lie beneath the surface, or in the decayed walls of mills or other buildings that stand in the water. When there is a bite, or run, you will feel a slight tug at the line, which should be held rather loose, you must then quietly withdraw the rod, and allow the Eel two minutes to gorge the bait; and then, by a sharp twitch, fix the needle across its throat; do not pull, but hold the line tight, and the Eel will soon make its appearance. A hook, No. 4 or 5, is frequently used in lieu of a needle.

HOW TO KNOW THE BIRDS

W. E. SAUNDERS, *TUXIS BOOK FOR BOYS* (1918)

❧ ❧

BIRD LIFE is attractive to every boy and no other hobby is more beneficial in its results. Even if it is followed casually, so that the total number of one's bird acquaintances amounts to perhaps twenty, zest and interest is added to every walk in the country or city and one is constantly renewing acquaintance with his feathered friends; and if, on the other hand, the hobby is pursued with enthusiasm, interest grows with the pursuit.

We all know that the bird is an animal that wears feathers, flies in the air, builds nests, lays eggs; but have you tried to learn anything of the details of the life of these interesting creatures? Do you know what birds prefer to fly, what birds prefer to walk, what birds prefer to

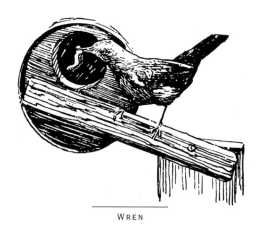

WREN

swim? Do you know what birds fasten their nests to frail twigs, which ones use larger limbs and crotches, and those using nesting sites around buildings or holes in trees? What birds nest on the ground, and which in holes in the ground? The number of questions that might be asked about these and similar phases of bird life is great, but your interest will be greater if you try to answer questions put by yourself, and you will not be able to ask these questions until you have started to make the acquaintance of some birds.

There are several easy and practical methods of getting acquainted with the birds at short range, any one of which may be used as a start. The easiest, perhaps, is the providing of nesting places. Providing food and drink is another method which leads to good results. In the summer time it is difficult to provide appropriate food for most birds, but greater numbers of them are attracted by water, which may be offered to them in various containers, from a simple pan laid on the ground, to an elaborate stone or concrete basin. It is also possible to get an intimate acquaintance with some birds by taking advantage of their nesting time to approach and make friends, but this is more difficult and takes much more time than inviting the birds to make friends with you. The great advantage of the latter method is that it may be pursued at your home and thus the birds are under constant observation.

The number of species that can be induced to nest in places made by human hands is small. The species most easily attracted is doubtless the house wren, whose bubbling song and familiarly inquisitive manner makes him perhaps the most welcome of all the summer sojourners. Wrens will nest in almost any sort of a cavity if they happen to fancy it, but in providing nesting sites for these wild

Robin nesting on the bird shelf

things it is better to approach nature as nearly as possible. Offer them a cavity nearly like the ones which have been used by their kind for hundreds of years, namely, the woodpecker hole. This is not a simple cylindrical hole in a piece of wood, but is shaped somewhat like a teardrop.

The natural excavation is here compared with that made by the best manufacturers, but it can be pretty well duplicated by splitting a short log and fastening the halves together after the hole is completed. Such houses, when placed in favorable situations, may attract not only the house wren but the flicker, woodpecker, blue bird, tree swallow, crested fly catcher, chickadee, and nuthatch, and while the first two species do not seem to be much attracted by any cavity except the standard natural one, those mentioned later may be induced to nest in almost any sort of a box.

It seems to be more within the reach of the human being to make friends with these hole-nesting birds than with a great many others, and that is a good reason for endeavoring to begin with birds of that type. Once a pair of birds is in-

DOWNY WOODPECKER
INSPECTING THE HOUSE

duced to nest in your garden, or around your home, the intimacy of your acquaintance with them is limited only by the amount of time you can spend with them.

Some other species of birds may be induced to nest on shelves put up for the purpose. These comprise the robin, phoebe, barn swallow, bronzed grackle, but the latter, with the cow bird and the blue-jay, are not good subjects for encouragement. They accept your efforts to lessen bird numbers by eating nestlings and eggs and it is a usual occurrence to find that where these predacious birds are encouraged, smaller and more useful birds diminish.

A little book by Samuel B. Ladd "How to Make Friends with the Birds" may be studied for additional information along this line.

Classification

As soon as you have made the acquaintance of even a few kinds of birds it is time to learn what families they belong to, for the reason that the habits of different species of a family are more or less alike. The robin, for instance, belonging to the thrush family, has habits which resemble to a considerable extent those of the hermit, wood and other thrushes. The habits of the song sparrow bear a close resemblance to those of other sparrows. The habits of the warblers, flycatchers, etc., bear close relation to each other, and as habits are often a strong clue to the identity of a bird, a knowledge of their relationship will be a valuable aid to identification.

Color is, of course, the usual key with which a bird's identity is made out, but habits are more instructive and interesting and should be studied as much as possible.

CHICKADEE

Bill

The most prominent point of resemblance in the different families of birds is the bill. The bill is the means of obtaining food and, therefore, it follows that the bill must carry a certain resemblance. Such families as woodpeckers, flycatchers, sparrows are good examples of families in which the bill is a real trademark, showing both occupation and relationship.

Color Variation

One phase of bird life which is very attractive and interesting to the beginner is the variation of coloring between the male and female birds. These variations are not confined to any special families, nor do they occur consistently throughout most, but very few families of birds fail to show such variations. Sometimes the differences are trivial, but often the male and female are so different that one would scarcely take them to belong to the same race. As a general rule it may be stated that those species which show the most brilliant colors show the greatest difference between the sexes.

Examples are the oriole, tanager, indigo bird, cardinal, bluebird, grosbeak, goldfinch and others.

Migrations

Birds, like human beings, have a home. It is the place where they return year after year to rear their young. The instinct for migration is developed to a wonderful extent. Set a boy down at Hamilton and tell him to walk to Guelph and he must ask his way many times, but the tiny hummingbird finds his way from Lake Superior across the Gulf of Mexico, and returns with no guide but that of instinct, which sense, it may be so called, is nearly dormant in human beings.

Nest Construction

One of the most interesting departments of bird study is the investigation of nest construction. After the young birds have flown, the nest may be taken and carefully picked to pieces, the pieces laid

BLUEBIRD, BLUE JAY

together in sorted piles and eventually counted. The individuality of birds may thus be studied, and if it should be possible to investigate the character of two or more nests made by one bird, the comparison may demonstrate the settled nature of the individual.

Big Birds

Every one ought to feel that in our birds, especially the larger ones, all the people have a common interest and proprietorship and it is the privilege of no one to kill wastefully or for display of prowess, any bird which belongs to the whole nation.

The larger the bird, the more widespread is the interest taken in it by the general public, and it must be regretfully stated that the larger the bird, the greater seems to be the impulse, on the part of a certain class of sportsmen, to kill it.

What feature could add so much to the interest of our waterways, for example, than the presence of numbers of fish hawks, herons and eagles, and the protection that they need depends largely upon the backing they receive from public sentiment. Every right-feeling boy will give his influence to the protection of these birds that need it so sorely.

WOODPECKER HOLE. PROTECTING
THE BIRD FROM CATS.

Protecting Life & Property: Safety on the Highways When Traveling

LT. COL. BARON DE BERENGER, *HELPS & HINTS* (1835)

❧ ❧

Y OUR "tools," or rather *weapons*, I shall first draw your attention to:

A stick, in able hands, is nearly as good as a sword, and in the hands of an inferior broad-swordsman, it is even better; there being but one edge to a cut and thrust sword (I mean from a few inches below the point, for, the latter has two edges), the cut is of no avail, unless made *with* the edge; whereas, the stick inflicts nearly equal pain, by a blow from *any* part of its circumference, wherefore, it has jocosely been called a sword having an edge all round. Nevertheless, the cut of a stick should be made similarly to that of a sword; that is, as *if it had* an edge, wherefore the line of cut or imaginary edge should always be as if in continuation of the line of the

middle joints of your fingers: by using your stick thus, you will hit rather harder, preserve your sword-play free from foul cuts, and you will also promote the action or suppleness of your wrist. A good mode is to draw a *narrow* chalk line upon the stick, and in the proper place of a sword's edge, thereupon to allow only such as cuts (during play with a fencing-school antagonist) as leave a chalk mark where the cut has been applied.

I recommend a stick of the former kind in preference; that is, of a weight suitable to the strength of the purchaser. My own fancy is in favor of the *blackthorn*; although a little more weighty than other saplings of the same dimensions, its many knobs help to save the knuckles more than a smooth stick. An *oak-sapling*, however, is an excellent stick, although not quite so tough as a blackthorn. Most of the other *canes* are too springy, both for parrying and also for making *true* cuts.

Good sticks should taper something more than they commonly do; the points should be strong, yet light enough to come up quickly; the ferules should be small and light, no more than just enough to protect the sticks from wearing, and they never should be allowed to be loose; the thickest or hand end should have a tendency to be oval, as laying more sword-like in the hand; and which should *not* grasp the stick tight, but ought to hold it lightly, and chiefly between the thumb and fore-fingers, the end of the other fingers giving increased momentum to the stick at the time of making a cut, the oval shape causing also the *supposed* edge to lay always in one and the same way: a leathern thong and tassel is necessary since, by passing your hand through it, and giving one or two twists of the stick, you can secure its retention by it, sword knot-like. A knob at the handle end is not only useless, but a definite impediment; and the loading of the end with lead is, if not absolutely cowardly, at the least foolish; for it deducts from the severity of a cut from the point; a loaded stick can only be used like a hammer, and then only at close quarters, for, by making a blow with the lead, and if removed only about two feet from the hand, the stick most likely will fly if parried, and if you miss your blow, you must expect to be knocked down before you can recover *so heavy* a point: one good parry to each will place the owners at his mercy. Attacks from a tuck stick being with its point, you have only to use almost any of the small sword *disarming* parries, quickly closing upon your assailant, at the same time, in order to seize his right with your left hand, and, after throwing the hilt end of your stick a little out of your hand, to strike it, with a backhanded blow, forcibly into his face or teeth, and as he staggers from you, to lay him at your feet, with either a severe cut at his head, or by giving point at his face, with the proper end of your stick.

If you wish to spare a tuck-stick assailant, one, who from inebriety, or from unaccountable folly, attacks you, you need but parry his thrusts, for very little force will avert them, *he* having the weighty end in front; and you may also keep him at arm's length, by giving point to his face sharply and repeatedly with your stick, and which, unless he is *much* longer armed than you, must keep his point off, since he cannot use it so well with one as with both his hands.

Prolix as my directions, in ref-

erence to so homely and so common a weapon, may have appeared to you, I can assure you that *your life may depend upon the toughness of your stick*; I recommend a perfectly sound one to you, although *my* life was saved even by my stick's breaking near the point, whilst applying a severe cut at the ribs of the most formidable of several footpads, whose ferocious attack gave me little hopes of extrication, nay, of life; it was saved, however, by mere chance, for, poising my broken stick, to ascertain its length, it being dusk, the powerful fellow, and who must have been a trooper, from his bludgeon skill, took it for a feint, and throwing himself open, by guarding his head, I seized the opportunity to give point at his face with the *splintered* end.

An umbrella even, on an emergency, may be converted into a weapon, provided the stick is sound, but only to give point; or it may be opened quickly, to serve as a shield to hide your pulling a pistol out of your pocket (taking care how you cock it *safely* with *one* hand), thereupon to shoot a robber, either through or under it, *taking great care to hit him*.

To prescribe the same rules of

resistance to all persons, without reflecting on the difference which must exist between them, as much in courage and presence of mind as in size, and therefore both in physical and in muscular powers, would be as ill-judged as the administering of the same medicine and doses to all constitutions indiscriminately would court reproach for madness; nevertheless, most, perhaps all, will agree upon this point.

Resistance to robbery not only is more manly than a tame submission to the dictates of a violator of his country's laws, and who therefore ought to be treated as one who is at war with all the civilized part of the community; but it also is more prudent, for you cannot fore-see what consequences your submission may heap upon you, besides loss by robbery. If the robbers are blood-thirsty, and therefore cowardly, submission most likely will seal your doom; whereas a determined resistance may be the only way to avert it; if, on the contrary, they should be brave, and which their illegal pursuit need not prevent, and if you should even be subdued by them, your display of courage will command more or less respect even from thieves, *provided they are not rank cowards*; whilst cowardice, although *they* gain by it, experiences the contempt of *all* plunderers, and provokes ill-usage, and degrading mortifications besides, and

from *every one*: Therefore, and at any rate, it must be preferable to employ brave and skillfully resisting efforts to avert maltreatment, than to experience such after all, although you have *not* resisted. Of course, persons not gifted with sufficient nerve, or those who are conscious of physical inability from corporeal defects, or from sickness, *such* persons, if attacked, had better refrain from resisting, for neither a pusillanimous attempt, nor one crippled by constitutional disability, can serve them, or the community, in any way; nevertheless, it is not in every case that weakness, inferiority in size, or the superiority of numbers, ought to be allowed to dishearten; since instances out of number can be given where determined boldness, activity, and presence of mind have succeeded even against awful odds, and solely because such were employed judiciously, although by mere lads, or even females. Remember—strength without courage is a treasure buried—strength without judgment is a giant shackled, but courage, presence of mind, and the *skillful* application of strength are impregnable bulwarks, that may defy and laugh to

scorn the laborings of superior, yet clumsy, force, and of brutal violence, deficient of refined courage.

Seize a pistol the moment when

it is presented at you, with one hand (but unless this can be done *neatly* it is better left alone) to force the muzzle either at his own, your assailant's, head, or, if that is impracticable, in any direction ensuring your own safety; at the same time, with your other hand, or rather well-clenched fist, hit him a sharp blow on the throat, but upwards, so as to be stopped by his chin, and with the nails of your fingers towards yourself (the back of the hand downwards), thus to make his heels fly up, taking care to avert the pistol from you in his fall, and which better, by a blow with your leg applied to the back of his, and as near to his heels as possible, you will make doubly sure; but unless you can apply this blow from your leg neatly, and in a way that ensures your remaining firm on your legs, *this part* had better be omitted, since you may throw *yourself* down, instead of your antagonist, or you may *fall with him*: secure his pistol and him when down, by kneeling on his throat, your face towards his pistol hand. All this refers to a case when, without any weapon, you have to rely on your fists; if you have a stick, seize the pistol as before, and throw the handle part of your stick to project a little *out* of your hand, to hit him with it a *back-handed* blow in the face.

Should you pass a fellow of suspicious appearance in a dangerous part of the road, do so without *seeming* to apprehend anything; nevertheless, watch him with a side glance out of the corner of your eyes, for it may enable you to catch a glimpse quickly, should he attempt (as is more than likely if he is a thief) to fell you, with a blow from behind; if you should discover such an endeavor, rapidly face about, throwing your stick up to the St. George's guard, at the same moment, and if you succeed

in making his blow slide off, immediately return a *severe* cut at his right ribs; or bring your right hand from the St. George's guard to a little above your right shoulder, as if about to make, although to appearance awkwardly, a cut at his head, but, *instead* of it, sharply and quickly to give point at his face, following these stabs up as long as he is under the control of your point. Probatum est!

Should members of the swell mob or other fellows have taken advantage of your carelessness so as to have succeeded in closely surrounding or hustling you, either with a view to confine your arms or to deduct from the force of your stick, by your being prevented from striking with your point, or that part near to it, which is the forte of your stick; *immediately* seize your stick *in the middle*, as it will enable you to hit or to parry with *either* end, not only in such a situation, but indeed whenever you are grappled by another, or at close quarters generally. If hemmed in thus by numbers, *thrust or poke* with *either* end at *any* of your assailants who lay themselves open; always doing it as *forcibly* and as rapidly as possible, and chiefly directing such pokes at their *faces* and *stomachs*, hitting occasionally, as opportunity offers, smart blows, which, however, from their contraction of the proper length, will not serve you so well as forcible thrusts. *Kick* the *shins* of such fellows at the same time smartly, especially of such as come *behind* you, and you may, by active and determined industry, soon make yourself an opening; for fellows attacking you thus otherwise will push and throw you to each other, in order to strip you of everything, and to cover you with bruises besides.

If you nimbly *can* fill your other hand, *in your pocket*, with the contents of your snuff-box, you cannot do better than by throwing some, but always with *a good aim and without waste* of such excellent ammunition, into the eyes of those *close* to you, to salute their heads with your trusty sapling at the same time: smarting under blindness and sneezing, they will open a gap *for you*, anxious as they will be to get away, whilst laboring under so perplexing a situation; and which, taking advantage of, will enable you to make good your retreat, carefully applying your "Irish blackguard" to those of the British breed that may endeavor to stop your exit; or *making belief* that your hand is full when the whole is gone: it requires, however, firmness and activity to effect this, and even to those possessed of both, my advice, is, to *avoid* getting into such clutches, by every precaution, as the only safe way with such hordes.

Precautions which ought to be attended to in walking the streets of great cities

Bear in mind that thieves, of whatever class, always prefer to make their attacks, or even their preparations for such, when they can make sure of some advantage: to lessen such advantages, by every precaution on your part, ought therefore to be your first care.

Accordingly, and as they secure the advantage of choosing the time, and the mode of attack, and as their taking you by surprise is, with them, a leading reliance, so it is necessary that you should *always* be prepared for them; at any rate you should take care neither by negligence nor weakness to lay yourself open to their taking advantage, and which either of these faults may, and most likely will, invite. Since *alert precaution is no more a confirmation of fear than foolhardiness is a proof of courage*, you ought not to disregard the advice of sound sense, for it will not fail to tell you, that it is less difficult, and therefore more rational, to avert an attack, than it is to repair the errors of carelessness, be it even by bravely, nay, dashingly subduing a robber, whom you have thus and so foolishly attracted.

Never therefore be off your guard, for vigilance is not fear!

If it should be a person's misfortune to be under the influence of timidity, let him carefully *conceal* his alarm, for its display invariably accelerates the attacks of assailants; just as the shrinking from a cur encourages him to bite, where a bold and firm handling, instead of shrinking, generally overawes animals. Do we not see daily that even timid curs will venture to pursue timid persons; and that a horse, almost instantly, will discover and take advantage of an agitated or nervous rider? As this proves that even animals probe our courage, to act accordingly, it cannot surprise us that the fear of *cap-*

ital punishment should cause a robber carefully to *observe*, and, in preference of all others, to *select* those persons whose *apparent* want of courage affords him a better chance of either success or escape.

To be courageous is enviable, whilst, on the other hand, to be able to conceal the absence of courage is useful.

Never walk with your *hands in your pockets*; move on carelessly, if in them you have anything of value, carefully avoid to betray anxiety by holding it, as if to guard it; nor should you feel occasionally, as if to satisfy yourself of its security, for these are the most certain ways whereby, to *attract* the notice of thieves; for, not only observing everything, as they do, they are sure to conclude from your care that the stake is as much worth an attempt on their part, as it is worth your while so anxiously to preserve it; they will even judge from your dress and general conduct whether you are, what they call "a good flat," that is, a weak-minded person, likely to be operated upon successfully.

Instead of allowing your tailor to make *outside pockets* to your

morning frocks or coats, order him to place them *inside*; and the addition of *a breast pocket*, large enough to admit a moderate sized pocket-book, is also desirable, as your *buttoning up* will increase its security in particular situations, and indeed that of the other pockets, more or less; nevertheless, you must not rely upon being secure, even then, for pickpockets are as crafty as they are nimble.

Avoid every unnecessary *display of money*, since no solid excuse can be offered for so dangerous an act of carelessness, or so pitiful a gratification of little-minded vanity. This practice is but too common with persons of weak intellect, or with perfect novices; and if, instead of being the result of thoughtlessness, their aim is to impress others with an idea of their consequence, it counteracts the very effect they endeavor to promote, for, just as every thinking observer concludes that the being the owner of a horse, or the master of a servant, must be something quite new with a person who more frequently than others introduces "my horse" or "my servant" into his conversation; so, to him, it cannot fail to become a confirmation that the possession of large sums must either be unusual or of recent date, with persons who so sillily can expose themselves to additional risks, by thus inviting and provoking the ingenuity of sharpers and thieves of every description.

The *bank, banking houses, army and navy agents*, or similar places which you may have occasion to frequent for the purpose of receiving money, should always be left in a more rational way than is pursued by many on leaving bankers' doors, and where you may see persons cramming handfuls of bank notes into pocket-books, in the very doorway even, or deposit cash bags about their dress as they walk along the street. When you have to receive money at such places, seek a position at the counter, as remote from the door as possible, *there* to count your money, and stow away your cash or pocket-book *before* you open the door. Where the sum is large, or the receiver is a stranger to the ways of London, to have a coach *in readiness* at the door is by far the wisest course. Similar precautions are applicable where you have to pay accounts at fashionable warehouses, etc.; for there, as well as at bankers' windows, nay, even those of pastry-cooks, pickpockets or

their scouts, disguised as beggars, servants, etc. are constantly on the look out, although less so since the police system has been perfected. Where you can settle your account in a counting house or a back shop it is always to be preferred.

The approaches to the *bank* about the time dividends are paid, the coffee houses, and even the shops and auction-rooms contiguous, swarm with a set of thieves and swindlers, seen there, and at these periods only, called "*dividend hunters*," whose object is, by all manner of ways (and some really of a serviceable and therefore ingratiating nature) to endeavor to draw you into conversation, into joining meals, or into joint purchases, or billiard or backgammon play for wine or money, or into betting upon political events, and by thousands of other schemes: they will speak of *each other* as persons of the highest respectability, and of great mercantile consequence; and these amiable communications they will whisper into your ear, if so foolish you are as to let them familiarize so much, to find at last that you might, with much the same kind of safety permitted if a boa constrictor were to coil itself about you, wherefore a stern yet inoffensive repulse is the only safe alternative, if necessity, in any way, should bring you in contact with persons at *such time and places*. Many of them are gentlemanly in their manners and address, and most are respectable in their appearance; but you are as sure to suffer in *some way or other* if you encourage them, as in a lower sphere of life any one will be sure to repent the folly of placing confidence in those fellows who, although so frequently exposed, nevertheless, succeed daily in paying *themselves* for the lessons they give to simpletons *how* to wrap up and safely stow away their money. There is very little difference between the characters and pursuits of these parties, for they differ in appearance only!

Instead of sauntering along town or its suburbs, *adopt* (unfashionable as it is) *a brisk and active pace*; especially if you have anything of great value about you. Thieves are as much baulked as puzzled by activity, as they are deterred by the probability of a spirited resistance; and which latter, from an active person, is more to be expected than from a loiterer,

since confidence and decision are allied to activity.

Always *avoid crowds*, whether occasioned by persons taken ill, or quarrelling, or fighting: four times out of five they are mere pretences, resorted to, to facilitate the plunder of the unwary votaries to curiosity.

A young friend of mine assured me that he was imposed upon, although a shrewd observer, in the following way: meeting a romping and noisy party of five or six very decently dressed young men, most of them tipsy in appearance; some abused the rest, and one even offered to fight them, "for using the gentleman so shamefully ill," whilst the others were particularly anxious to make amends by busily wiping my friend's clothes with their handkerchiefs, all the while apologizing in terms of respectful regret, expressed in decent language. My liberal and good-tempered friend, finding these lads as sorry as attentive, and unwilling that a fight should grow out of his misfortune, did all he could to appease the anger of his defenders; and what with the wiping, sponging, and rubbing down, and the being tugged about, some of the young fellows forcing their names and addresses upon him all the while, as well as their apologies, the cards being those of decent tradesmen, he had so much to do and to think of, that he never thought of his pockets. They entreated, nay insisted, upon his going into a public-house, close by, to wash his face, and "to be made decent, with more comfort" than could be done in the street and, as it were, "killing him with kindness," they pushed him in before them, at the same time calling out to those behind, "Stop, Dick and Tom, you must not go; come in!" leaving the house suddenly with such calls, as if to bring them in, but also leaving my young-friend *solus*, and *minus* too of everything his pocket had contained but a few minutes previously. "Knowing" as my friend was considered to be, he declared that the whole was acted so cleverly, that he scarcely could believe even the evidence which his empty pockets so confirmingly presented. The cards of course were those of honest persons, but strangers to the whole of the parties, and to the transaction.

Never pull out your watch to satisfy any inquirer, but tell him the time by guess, continuing your walk all the while: besides the risk of having a watch snatched from you, and which is not infrequently practiced, your holding it prevents your using that hand if you should be attacked, and which the inquirer may contemplate.

If asked questions about the road, or any street, or the name of any resident, or if any gay lady should try to force her conversation on you; either *turn a deaf ear to the party*, or, to fair inquiries, reply carelessly; and briefly, as if in a hurry or behind time: Improper importunities avert sternly, even roughly, yet not offensively, and, in each of these cases, always without halting! Large parcels have been placed in gentlemen's hands, with a request to indulge the bearer, who professed to be "no scholar," by reading the address to him; and whilst the condescending gentleman was puzzled how to make out for the homely-looking porter some ill-written address, his pockets were emptied, either by the porter himself, shielded by the parcel, or by his allies. For many reasons, of which the following alone is a sufficient one, never let *fair strangers*, who may accost you in the streets, under pretended acquaintance, or other excuses, lay hold of your arm: shake them off with a bow, and the assurance that they are mistaken, and cross the road directly; nay, as these *ladies* very frequently "hunt in couples," they may endeavor to honor you by attempts to take you between them, by each seizing upon one of your arms; if so, you cannot give them a better proof of your becoming sensibility of their kindness than by adopting their very ideas; I mean by thinking even as *they do just then*, that is,—of your pockets!

Much easier is it to advise you *how* to *keep out* than to *get out*, of *such* a scrape! At any rate, should your endeavors prove successful (and which is subject to doubt,) exposure and degradation will inseparably be yours.

"*Duffers,*" as an impudent set of vagabonds are called, are also carefully to be avoided. They mysteriously offer "*smuggled*" valuable shawls, or lace, or indeed any article liable to a heavy duty, or watches and trinkets, yet for very trifling prices, under pretence of wanting money, or of being overstocked. Never listen to them one moment, sternly bid them go about their business, and insist upon it too, in the hearing of passengers; for, at the best, and if you could be so mean as to buy of

them, their goods, instead of being smuggled, are of British manufacture, showily, but defectively got up, and purposely *to deceive*; even gold watches very splendid and good to appearance, are hawked in that sort of way.

Wanton assaults, either to gratify vulgar insolence, or to lead to a quarrel, perhaps to facilitate robbery, are practiced mostly under the guile of *assumed* intoxication. When you see *a fellow staggering towards you*, whether really drunk or pretending inebriety, give him all the room you can; take no notice of anything he may say or do, nor stop even to look, but proceed on as if you had not even seen him. Should he endeavor to save himself from falling by an attempt to seize hold of you (a common trick with thieves), slip cleverly from his grasp; his manner of saving himself thereupon will soon show you that he knows perfectly well *what* he is about.

Persons running along the streets with speed, more commonly willfully than otherwise, will encounter you with a great shock: not only may you avert this, but even visit it upon the aggressor, by nimbly moving forward the point of that shoulder which is *nearest to him* to receive the shock, and by throwing all your weight to support that point; to be effected by a sudden but firm inclination of your body that way, and rather forward; doing it neatly, and just at the very time when he is about to come in contact with you, will warrant your confidently looking for him in the kennel, unless he is a person very much heavier than yourself; it is more easy still, if he has just turned a corner, a mode generally adopted by rogues after having reconnoitered your approach.

This essay originally contained several *other* powerful modes of resistance, and also some most *destructive* ways of defeating ferocious assailants; but, as these instructions, and, in reality, master-tricks, might be used in furtherance of felonious attacks, the author thought it his duty to *suppress* their publication, rather than to endanger the Public; yet he is perfectly willing to impart them to pupils, trusting that *they* will not allow them to transpire, so as to reach improper characters.

FRIED APPLES FOR HUMAN FOOD

SERONO EDWARDS TODD, *APPLE CULTURIST* (1871)

❧ ❦

IN THOSE regions where potatoes are few and poor, on account of the rot, fried apples are an excellent substitute. They are quickly prepared for the table, which is often a consideration of no small importance. Wash them, cut them in two, take out the stem, core, and calyx, and, unpeeled, put them into a tin pan with butter, or the gravy of baked pork, with some water, in proportion to the quantity to be fried; cover them with a lid, set them on the stove, stir them occasionally until they become soft, and be careful not to burn them.

Romanites, which are often almost worthless, baked or raw, "disappear with good gusto when fried." We may truthfully pronounce despicable Penics good, when fried; but the Porters, Bellflowers, Talman's Sweeting, and a long list which we might name, when fried, are really a luxury.

Most persons like apples in a raw state, or when they are baked or stewed; and it can not be denied that they furnish one of the most wholesome and agreeable kinds of diet. Although raw, stewed, or baked apples may be pronounced excellent and delicious, still there are many kinds, when fried, which are super-excellent; and they who seldom meet with a dish of fried apples often wonder why they are not always fried instead of baked. When apples are baked, they often burst open, and much of the best part flows out as juice, and is lost. But when they are fried, the whole is saved. In our own family we consume five or six barrels of apples before one barrel of Irish potatoes is gone. Many persons who do not care to eat more than one or two crude apples per day, will often eat six or eight when they are fried.

The want of a natural appetite is the result of the bile not being separated from the blood; and if not remedied, fever is inevitable, from the slightest grades to that of bilious, congestive, and yellow fever. But those persons who eat large quantities of crude or cooked apples are never troubled with constipation or biliousness. An incalculable amount of sickness and suffering would be prevented every year, if apples were employed to a greater extent on our tables, instead of such immense quantities of heavy animal food. Good beef, mutton, oysters, and roasted fowls make excellent living; yet, in many instances a dish of fried apple will operate like magic in giving a healthful tone to the whole system of a high-living dyspeptic.

By an arrangement of Providence as beautiful as it is benign, the fruits of the earth are ripening during the whole summer. From the delightful strawberry, on the opening of spring, to the luscious peach of the fall, there is a constant succession of superb aliments; made luxurious by that Power whose loving kindness is in all his works, in order to stimulate us to their highest cultivation, connecting with their use also the most health-giving influences.

Liebig says, they prevent debility, strengthen digestion, correct the putrefactive tendencies of nitrogenous food, avert scurvy, and strengthen the power of produc-

tive labor. If eaten frequently at breakfast, with coarse bread and butter, without meat or flesh, apples have an admirable effect on the system, often removing constipation, correcting acidities, and cooling off febrile conditions more effectually than the most approved medicines.

HOW TO FLY

A. FREDERICK COLLINS, *HOW TO FLY* (1917)

❧ ❧

FLYERS ARE in great demand. The United States Government wants men for its flying corps and you can be one of them.

To be an airman in time of war is not only less dangerous than fighting in the trenches but it is far more exciting, and, besides, it puts you in the front rank to win honor and glory.

Though it is not hard to learn to fly, there are but few who can handle an aeroplane at the present time; hence to be a pilot *now* means in a literal sense that you are a superman, for you are above your earth-bound fellows, at least when you are winging your way through cosmic space.

Now you may or may not know it, but the aeroplane is the speed machine of today.

It has been highly developed to meet the exacting and rigorous conditions imposed by the present war, and when the great conflict is over, manufacturers will direct their energies toward supplying the need for sporting and commercial machines.

Aeroplanes, as they are now designed, constructed, and flown, are as safe, or safer, than automobiles, nor does it take much more mental and physical energy to learn to drive them, but what it does take to fly is the kind of stuff that men are made of.

To be a flyer at this stage of the game will put you in the front rank of the birdmen, for the art is new and history is long.

Therefore I say unto you: Learn to fly now. Leave this mundane spheroid under you and make short cuts over the hills and rivers and whatever other obstacles have heretofore impeded your two-dimensional travel, and go in an air line.

This is the age of the swift, by the swift, and for the swift; and the aeroplane is the last word in progressive achievement. Your opportunity to learn to fly is at hand today, so do it *now* and be ready to go to the front in an escadrille.

How an Aeroplane Flies

I will tell you in a few words just how an aeroplane flies, so that you will have a clear idea of what the rest is all about as you come to it.

Make this experiment: take a board 6 or 8 inches wide and 3 or 4 feet long and strike the still surface of the water in a pond with the flat side of it and you will find that it acts as though it were a *solid body* instead of a *yielding fluid* at the moment the board hits it. Now it is the same way with the air; if you strike it hard enough with the flat side of a board, or a plane, it acts as though it is nearly solid, at the instant of impact, instead of just thin air.

A kite, or the wings of an aeroplane, is set at an angle so that when it is in flight the air strikes the under surface of the planes; this deflects—that is, turns the air down—and it is this force of the planes striking the air, or the air striking them, or both together, that keeps the machine from falling for a given moment, but it would fall the next moment if it were not for the *high speed* at which it is driven and which makes the planes keep on striking the air and so hold it up.

About the Air

There is much more to the mixture of gases surrounding the earth, which we call the air, than we can see of it, and it allows many things to be done that could not be done if there were no such thing as air. Flying is one of them.

What the Air Is Made Of.— The air, or *atmosphere*, as it is sometimes called, is simply a mixture of 1/5 part of oxygen, 3/4 part of nitrogen, and 1/20 carbon dioxide with small traces of other gases making up the rest of it; and altogether it absorbs a lot of water vapor.

The Air Has Weight.— Though the air is made up of gases it has weight, and so the air at the top presses down the air which rests on the surface of the earth; the *pressure* of the air at sea level is, in round numbers, 15 pounds to the square inch, and of course the air is more dense, or compressed, at the bottom than it is at the top.

The Height of the Air.—As the eagle cannot fly higher than 3 or 4 miles, it is not likely that the aeroplane will beat this record by more than a mile or two. A balloon once ascended to a height of 7 miles, but the air was so thin that the aeronauts became unconscious.

It is believed that the definite limit of the air is reached at a height of about 50 miles and that at this height it has a surface like that of the ocean. On this surface great billows of air roll to enormous heights, and from the observation of shooting stars it is known that there are traces of air to a height of 200 miles or more.

How to Become a Pilot

And now the time draws near when you will learn how to fly. What I intend to try to do is to tell you how to learn to fly and obtain your pilot's license in the shortest possible time and with the least possible danger.

It is said that there are a few

people who could never learn to ride a bicycle, and it is certain there are some people who couldn't learn to walk a tight rope or be a steeple-jack. So, too, there are a few fellows who haven't the mental make-up which would permit them to fly with safety.

There are five things you ought to have if you are to become an expert aviator, and these are: (1) youth, (2) natural aptitude, (3) good sense, (4) knowledge, and (5) confidence. In my estimation, youth is of the least importance, and confidence is of the greatest.

Youth.—To begin with, you should be young, for this means that you will be apt to learn the new tricks of the air easily, but on the other hand you should not be too young. Choosing one's age, however, is very like choosing one's parents—you can't always do it.

While there are a few licensed pilots who are only 18 or 19 years of age, you should not learn to fly until you are 20 at least. Nor should you learn to fly after you are 35, although this may be putting the age limit a little too low, for many men have learned who are past the 50 mark.

I'll qualify what I have said

above by adding that the younger men usually learn to fly much easier and quicker than those who are middle aged.

To do the right thing at the right instant without having to think about it is what is meant by natural aptitude, and human beings are born with this power, as well as the lower animals.

Natural aptitude in flying means that you have the ability to keep your aeroplane right side up and level under all conditions by pulling a lever, pushing a foot-bar, or turning a wheel at the instant needed and without having to think about it.

Good Sense.—However well you may have developed your natural aptitude it is not enough in itself to make you a good aviator; you must help it over the more difficult places with good, sound sense—that is, if you expect to fly another day.

An aviator having good sense will not attempt to fly when the wind is so high or so gusty that he knows it is not safe to go up. Of all the accidents which aviators have met with, between 80 and 85 per cent were caused by high winds. It is the fellows who fly in gusty winds, make steep dips, turn sharp curves, loop-the-loop, and do other spectacular but useless stunts who come to grief.

But using good sense does not begin and end when you are flying. You need it when you are making a getaway if there are trees or other obstacles in the way, in the air when some little thing goes wrong, and in landing when you will have to pick out the right place and gauge distances.

With all their other flying qualities put together, plus good machines but minus good sense, Wright and Curtiss and other pilots like them could not have kept up their flights these many years and still stay in the class of those who fly with engine-driven wings. Be like them and use good sense, and flying will be as safe as driving a motor boat or automobile.

Knowledge.—If you have studied up on the subject of mechanical flight you will be greatly helped not only when you take the controls of a machine in your hands for the first time, but ever afterward, though you may not realize it.

To know how your machine is built and balanced, how the engine works and what it can and might do, about the air when it is at rest and in motion and what its effect on your aeroplane is apt to be under varying conditions, are products of learning that are of the greatest importance, but ones that are too often overlooked by beginners and sometimes by the older fliers.

Confidence.—A person whose knees knock together whenever he looks out of a sixty-story window or who is afraid to climb to the top of an 800-foot mountain has no business with an aeroplane.

An aeronaut who can hang by his toes from the trapeze bar of a balloon while it is going up at the rate of 400 feet a minute, cut his parachute loose when he is up a mile or so and drop 1,000 feet before it opens has an over-supply of aeronautical nerve, and looping-the-loop would be too tame for him.

But fortunately there is a happy medium between these extremes of timidity and fool-hardiness, and nearly everyone is so mentally balanced that he has all the necessary courage to fly and yet no desire to risk his life uselessly in so doing.

Flying, though, is like every-

thing else that seems risky to an onlooker—it soon gets to be common and everybody will get used to it just as they get used to motoring. Whatever may be your thoughts and feelings before you make a flight for the first time, the moment you realize that you are really flying you know that at last you are above the world and all of its dangers.

And as you get off the ground and speed through space you feel the thrill of a new sensation surging through your blood and you wish you could keep right on flying. From this time on, wherever you are, you will hear the call of the air and it will sound good to you.

To make a good pilot, then, you must have a large supply of confidence both in yourself and in your machine. If this is tempered with good sense and you have a natural aptitude for flying, you will be fit to join the great flock of birdmen and to share the freedom of the air with them.

Skill.—While you may have a fair share of natural aptitude, may be gifted with a large measure of good sense, may be possessed of much knowledge, and have all the confidence an aviator needs to be a really skillful pilot, you must be able to correlate them; that is, make them work together just as though they were a lot of cogwheels meshing with each other.

And, what is more, not only must these factors work smoothly together, but they must do so just as though it were second nature with you. Yet with all of these things you will not be counted skillful unless you can bring quick action to bear when it is needed. An astronomer may be skillful and work slowly, but an aviator, to be skillful, must be able to work fast.

Measure yourself by the standards I have set and you can readily figure out whether or not you will make a successful pilot.

How to Learn to Fly

There are two ways open for you to learn to fly, and these are: (1) by teaching yourself; and (2) by joining an aviation school.

Training Camps.—The easiest and safest way is the last-named way, and as the tuition, that is, the amount you pay for taking a course at a training camp, is usually deducted from the cost of a machine if you buy one, this is the cheapest and best way in the end.

Quite a number of companies maintain schools and flying fields and have practice machines that are fitted with dual controls so that both you and the pilot who instructs you have a wheel at the same time and you learn to fly the machine with a minimum of danger.

After you have learned the things that are set down in this book you will be well prepared to take a course at the training camp. Under these conditions, if you are an apt pupil, you will only need to fly half an hour a day for a week until you can get your pilot's license.

Routine Method.—Whether

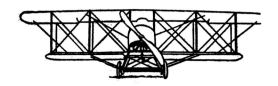

DUAL CONTROL IN AN OLD WRIGHT MODEL

you are learning to fly by yourself or at a camp, the first thing you should do is to go over the machine and understand every detail of its construction, and you should know the engine, too.

Next, you take your seat and have the men start the engine, which they do by turning the propellers round; then the men hold the machine to keep it from getting away from you until you are ready and say, "Let her go."

First you run the machine along the ground like a windwagon, and you need a big level field to do it on, for you steer it with the rudder. When you get this control down fine, run the machine on the ground and balance it on one wheel; this will quickly teach you how to warp the wings, shift the ailerons, or control the elevating planes.

Starting Up.—As soon as you are able to do the above things you will have no trouble in flying; indeed your greatest difficulty will be not to fly.

In starting to make an actual flight, turn your machine so that it faces the wind. Climb into your seat and have your helpers hold on until you are ready to start. Give your engine plenty of gas, and when your propellers are turning at their top speed you signal to let her go.

As you run along the ground your aeroplane gathers speed until finally the tail lifts from the ground a little, as shown. Then you tilt the elevating plane and the nose of your machine goes up and you leave the ground so gently you would not know it except that the riding is smoother. Then up and away; your modern pterodactyl (an extinct flying reptile and the largest living thing that ever flew) soars as high and as far as your heart desires—or, at least, as you and it can stand.

Making a Landing.—To fly is easy, but it's the landing that sometimes hurts. At first you should only make short, straightaway

flights and keep within a few feet of the ground.

Whenever you are making a landing, always keep your engine running and see to it that your machine faces the wind. If you stop your engine just before you touch

the earth your machine may fall, and if you land with the wind at your back it may tip over on its nose.

When Flying.—When you have learned to land, which is the hardest part of the whole art of flying, and have grown skillful in handling your aeroplane on short, straightaway flights, you are ready to try your head and hand at turning, and you begin by making large curves.

Just as a train must tilt inward, on rounding a curve, to keep it from jumping the track, so an aeroplane must be tilted inward, or banked, as it is called, when you turn it, or it will lose its sidewise balance and take a tumble.

When the machine is banked the wings offer a smaller lifting surface than when they are level, that is, horizontal with the earth's surface; then the inside wing, since it moves slower than the outside wing, begins to sink, and if you are not careful it will go farther down than you intended and keep right on slipping.

To right it you warp the outside wing or raise the inside aileron, which gives the inside wing a larger surface than the out-

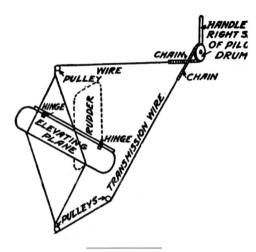

EARLY WRIGHT CONTROL. DOTTED LINE SHOWS THE RUDDER.

side wing, and this brings the machine back to its proper position again. It is this control of the wings, or ailerons, which will give you a good chance to show your natural aptitude and a few other personal qualities.

All machines should be fitted with an incidence indicator, one of which is shown. This indicator enables a flyer—be he pupil or pilot—to know the angle of his machine with relation to the surface of the earth, and hence he can always be sure of remaining in a safe flying position.

The Glider, or Volplane.— When you have become thor-oughly proficient in making figure eights, you have one more thing to learn before you can qualify for a pilot's license and that is to glide, or volplane, to the earth with your engine shut off.

The best way to do this is to head the machine toward the earth at its natural gliding angle before you stop the engine. When the machine has gathered speed, steer it so that its path will be a great spiral. If you can start your motor you can, of course, straighten up your aeroplane and steer it as you will again; but if it is dead the only thing you can do is to make a landing.

When your machine is within 100 feet of the ground tilt up your elevating plane and this will make it nose up a bit and glide off at a tangent, as shown, and as you are more nearly parallel with the ground you can strike it very gently. You can't make this kind of landing, though, if the machine isn't going fast enough.

When you are flying it is a good scheme always to keep the tail of your machine a trifle higher than its nose, so that should your engine go dead when you are not expecting it, your aeroplane will already be pointed down ready for a glide; otherwise it might lose headway and fall to the earth tail first.

The reason the volplane is added to the other tests required to get a pilot's license is so that you will know what to do when your engine stops suddenly. The main thing is to keep your nerve and bring your skill to bear and you will make the glide to earth safely.

High Flying.—It is much safer to fly high than it is to fly low, for while the wind usually blows harder, the higher you get, the steadier it is. Another thing: by flying high you have more time

and a longer distance in which to bring your machine to the gliding angle should your supply of gasoline give out and your engine stop, and for the same reason it is easier to choose a good place to land, especially if you are flying over a city.

Buying a Machine.—When you have learned to fly you will have some very clear-cut ideas on the kind of a machine you want. Should you intend to get a machine and then learn to fly don't fool yourself into the belief that you can design and build one yourself that will be better or cheaper than those sold in the open market.

No, you can't do it even if you are a mechanical engineer with an M.E. tacked after your name and you have skilled workmen at your beck and call. What you ought to do is to learn to fly first and then buy a machine from some good reliable maker, for in this way you will have money in pocket and keep your soul and body together a little longer than by doing everything yourself.

By flying first and buying a machine afterward, you will have a much better idea of what you want and what you can get than if you buy first and then fly. However, it is well to remember that a biplane is safer than a monoplane in virtue of the additional pair of wings and the fact that they are joined together by stanchions.

If all of your flying is to be done over land or your landing place is the ground, get an aeroplane mounted on a chassis with wheels. If you live on a lake or a river and you can use these for starting and alighting, a flying boat is the ma-

The Speed of an Aeroplane

As the speed of all things that move on the surface of the earth is measured by the time taken for them to travel a certain distance, when men began to fly the speed of aeroplanes was figured out in the same way.

Now the speed of an aeroplane depends not only on its own power but on the strength and direction of the wind in which it is moving, and not on the ground over which

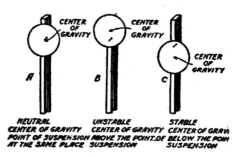

chine to get.

Then you have to choose between a machine that is a tractor and one that is a pusher. For purposes of learning, an ordinary pusher biplane is better than a tractor, as the latter is built more especially for scouting and military work.

it is flying. Say, for instance, that the wind is blowing 25 miles an hour and the aviator in his machine is moving against it at 25 miles per hour, then to an observer on the ground it would seem that the machine is standing still.

But if the wind is blowing 25 miles an hour and the aviator is moving with it at a speed of 25 miles an hour, it would seem to the observer on the ground that the machine is making 50 miles an hour. In calculating the speed of an aeroplane, the strength and the direction of the wind must always be taken into account.

Finding Your Way Through the Air

In flying it is often very hard to know just where you are, though you may know the lay of the land well enough when you are traveling on it.

A bird's-eye view of the country in flying over it is a new and strange sight to the eyes of mankind. The best way to find your course through the air is by the use of maps which show the chief landmarks and the best places to make a landing.

An air compass is indispensable for long-distance flying. In this type of compass the bowl is supported in the binnacle on three rubber-covered trunnions which, together with a quantity of horse-hair packing in the bottom of the binnacle bowl, absorbs all vibration; this gives a very steady card.

Useful additions to the compass are a magnifying prism and having the card graduations painted with luminous paint. The prism enables the compass to be located on a level with the eye, which gives perfect clearance for operating the controls; and the luminous card also obviates the

CURTISS TRACTOR TRIPLANE

uncertainty of electrical illumination.

It is necessary, however, to equip the compass with an electric lamp, which will give all the light needed on one dry cell. This light is needed only at twilight, when it is not dark enough for the luminous paint to show the card clearly.

Other Things to Know

There are, of course, a few other things to be learned about flying, but they will come to you without effort when you have made a few flights by yourself. When you can fly well enough to get your pilot's license you can consider that you are in very truth a birdman.

The tests for the Royal Aero Club's brevet are two series of five figures of eight each round two given marks. At the end of each series a landing has to be made within 50 yards of a given mark. In addition, a third flight has to be made to a height of not less than about 400 feet and a descent effected with the engine completely cut off.

Many people only take about three or four hours' actual flying before they take their tickets. That is certainly quick, but I think a good ticket should be taken after

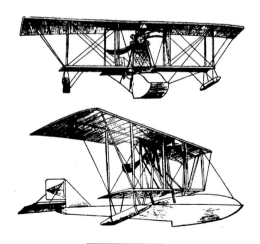

THE DONNET-LEVEQUE FLYING BOAT—FRONT AND SIDE VIEW

six or seven hours in the air.

It must be clear that a newly certified pilot has but very little experience. All beginners will do well to realize this and appreciate that they have just begun. A boy who has just taken his ticket is naturally very pleased with himself, and thinks there is nothing about aviation that he does not know. It is a great mistake and sometimes, alas, a fatal one. Always remember in aviation that you learnt to walk before you could run.

I think it may be appropriate to add a few words with regard to clothing. There are such a large number of disguises on the market that the intending aviator may experience some difficulty in making his choice.

Unless the pilot is comfortable in his machine, he will become fidgety and his attention will be slightly disturbed. To be comfortable then is a necessity. Comfort can only be attained by being properly clothed. Even in summer and at only a few hundred feet it is rather cold work sitting still in an aeroplane, while in winter the cold becomes really acute.

A warm coat should always be worn. Not necessarily leather, but something in which one's movements are free and easy. Leather, of course, has a special advantage in certain tractor machines where oil is flowing freely.

The hands and feet are perhaps the easiest target for the cold, so particular care should be devoted to obtaining a really comfortable warm pair of gloves.

I personally recommend leather gauntlet gloves, with some form of woolen lining; but the leather should be sufficiently soft to allow the fingers and wrists to move freely. They must also be large enough without being clumsy.

Warm socks or stockings are essential to keep the feet warm. A great many pilots like to fly in gun boots. But here again the same principle applies. Something warm, sufficiently large to be comfortable, without being too large to fit on the rudder bar.

The head and ears want protecting with a woolen or leather (wool-lined) cap.

If no wind screen is provided, goggles must be worn. This is important. At first you may find that your eyes get used to the rush of air and do not water. However, the perpetual strain on the eyes is bound to tell, and trouble will ensue. If you are lucky enough to have strong eyes and good sight, remember they were given to you to use and not to abuse.

If flying a tractor machine whose engine throws back much oil, take a small piece of chamois leather to wipe your goggles with. It is no use smearing the glass with gloves or a handkerchief; it only makes matters worse. In most machines of to-day, efficient wind screens are provided which do away with the necessity of goggles.

Before starting off across country, it is as well to make certain that you have enough petrol and oil in your tanks. In addition, a certain number of tools, a sparking plug or two, some wire, etc., should be carried. Your map, with route clearly marked, must be placed so that you can read it in comfort. The engine must be run on the ground to your entire satisfaction. It is never worth while commencing a flight with an engine that is not doing its best. Get to a reasonable height over the aerodrome before leaving its vicinity.

A few words now with regard to finding one's way.

It is most necessary to have a good map of the whole course. I personally think 1/4" Ordnance Survey is the most suitable map for ordinary cross-country work. The

course should be clearly marked and the map arranged in its case. Owing to limitations of space and weight you will find very few map-cases more than about 9 inches long. This then allows of about 36 miles on the map being visible at any one time. The roller map-case overcomes this difficulty, as a long length of map can be put on the rollers. As the pilot advances along his course he can keep pace on the map by turning one of the rollers.

Provided that the ground is visible, the whole course should be followed on the map. Certain objects stand out very clearly, and these should always be looked for. Water is perhaps the best guide to the aviator. Canals, rivers, and reservoirs prove of the greatest assistance. Railways too stand out very clearly in open country. Even in enclosed country they are usually to be found from the smoke of a passing train. Roads are apt to be rather deceptive, especially in England, where there are so few straight stretches; furthermore, there are many miles of roads concealed by trees; and unimportant roads in existence that are not marked on the map. Main roads, if they are covered with tarmac, are not nearly so visible as the second-class macadamed road.

In any flight that you are likely to undertake you are almost sure to find either a river, canal, or railway along a greater part of it. If you do not happen to have one of them to follow, you will be continually cutting them, then you can check your exact position on the map. Towns and large forests, being visible from a long distance, are also of great assistance.

In addition, the course should throughout be checked by compass bearing. It is most necessary to make allowance for a side (or partially side) wind when using the compass. For example, an aeroplane traveling from A to B (B being west of A) in a northerly wind has to steer considerably north of west to counteract the effect of the wind.

If the exact strength and direction of the wind were known for the height at which a flight is to be made, the necessary allowance could easily be calculated from an ordinary parallelogram of forces. As the wind is such a variable quantity, this is not a very practical method. The best way to make the necessary allowance is as under:

Climb to a height at which you intend to fly, over the aerodrome; start exactly over the aerodrome in a direction along your course. There is almost certain to be some prominent object within view along this course; about 5 miles would be a suitable distance. Steer direct at this point and note the compass reading, which will be the correct one for that course. On changing course the procedure should be repeated.

Such a method is, of course, only wholly possible when flying below the clouds. If a flight is to be made entirely above the clouds, the necessary allowance for wind must be calculated. Meteorological reports should be available at any

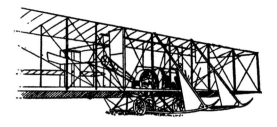

A GYRO ENGINE MOUNTED IN A WRIGHT BIPLANE

aerodrome, giving the strength and direction of the wind at various heights. Failing this, the strength and direction of the wind at ground level can be read from an anemometer and deduced for any other height. Under such circumstances it is essential to have the compass accurately adjusted to counteract deviation, and to make proper allowance for variation.

Although not advocating this method of finding a compass course, it should be possible to get within 5 or 10 degrees of the required direction. As already explained, the accuracy of the calculation should be tested by a regular descent below the clouds.

I now come on to the rather thorny question of forced landings. To land a machine where one wants and in an orderly manner is by far the most difficult part of

flying. When forced to descend across country, there is the further difficulty of determining where one does want to land. As soon as the engine stops it becomes necessary to choose a landing-place.

Provided one has a sufficient margin of height, there is time to look round and make a careful selection. There is of necessity a great element of uncertainty when choosing a ground from above.

It must be borne in mind that an aeroplane will only land on certain surfaces. The ordinary aerodrome is grass covered, and short grass does perhaps form the most suitable surface possible. However, when forced to descend in strange country, if you decide on a grass field, make certain it is grass. Roots and unripe corn are also green, and at any height are very difficult to distinguish from grass.

Then there is grass and grass. Uncut hay presents the same disadvantages to the aviator as corn does. It is almost impossible to land a machine in corn or long grass, because the wheels and skids (if any) will catch in it and cause the machine to turn over its nose on to its back. It might be possible for a very skillful pilot to land certain machines in corn without turning over, but the landing would have to be so slow that the machine had practically lost all forward way. It would, in fact, be a "pancake" landing, which would very likely break the undercarriage.

If you do find yourself about to settle in corn, you must of course pancake, the possibility of a broken undercarriage being by far the lesser evil than a cartwheel over the nose of the machine.

Then again, suppose one did effect a successful landing in crops, it would be impossible to get out of them without beating down a track for the machine to run along. Material damage of that kind should always be avoided. So from every point of view avoid landing in crops.

On a windy day it should be possible to spot long grass or corn, as the wind sets up a wavy motion.

In the fall of the year, when the corn has been cut, stubble forms an excellent surface. Ploughed ground is quite possible, but great care must be taken to settle very slowly. Where the furrows are more than usually deep it should be avoided.

As the surface of an unknown ground is such an uncertain quantity, it is of the first importance to see that its surroundings make a descent feasible. For instance, do not select a ground surrounded by trees—unless the landing-ground is particularly large; it is always most difficult to alight on it successfully over trees.

An efficient machine dived steeply on such an occasion will have acquired an enormous speed by the time it is flattened out. The result will be a collision with whatever there happens to be at the other end of the field. A normal glide over trees will bring a machine a long way across the field before it touches the ground at all. The result will be similar in either case.

For the same reason, fields surrounded by houses or other buildings should be avoided. Whenever possible then, make for open country.

Then again, the shape of the field selected is of the utmost importance. Some fields are long and narrow; such a field is quite all right provided the wind is blowing approximately up or down it. It is, however, a mistake to try and land in the length of a long field if a strong side wind is blowing.

It is always essential to land as nearly into the wind as possible. Try then and select a field whose lengthways happens to be against the wind. The direction of the wind is best indicated by smoke; this should always be looked for.

The next consideration is the slope of the ground. Gentle slopes are not easily discernible from a height, but they should be carefully watched for. A steep-ish slope should be detected without much difficulty. River valleys will help to give a general indication of the lie of the land. Flat ground should always be tried for. If only sloping ground is available, select a patch which can be approached uphill and against the wind.

In the same way, if plough is the only ground within reach, select a place where the plough is cut up and down the particular direction of the wind—that is to say, land along the plough provided it is also against the wind.

On all occasions select a place where misjudgment will have the least evil consequences. For example, do not select the edge of a precipice or even the sides of a railway cutting.

It is of course more convenient to land near a road if help is required. Such a consideration, however, should be taken into account after all others. Do not risk a smash in order to get near a road. When landing over a road or rail-

way, bear in mind that there are almost certain to be telegraph wires to land over. Now, telegraph wires are invisible from above, but the poles are not. Always keep a sharp look out for the latter when making a descent near a road or railway.

A few general hints may prove of value to the uninitiated.

Firstly always take a little money when flying across country. You will find it very useful if forced to descend in strange parts.

A smoke and a match may prove of some comfort to the smoker who has to survey the remains of his erstwhile flying machine!

Even nowadays the sight of an aeroplane still attracts a large crowd of inquisitive yokels. Try and prevent them from breaking up the machine, or even its remains, if you do have to land in the country. If possible a local policeman should be put in charge of it while you go and telephone for

A U.S. BATTLEPLANE WITH A LEWIS MACHINE GUN MOUNTED ON THE BOW

A CURTISS FLYING BOAT

help.

If the machine has to be left out all night, it should be wheeled to the most sheltered corner of the field, placed head to wind, and pegged down. Screw pickets are the best things to use as pegs. The machine should then be picketed down at both wheels and at each wing tip. In addition the tail should be secured to the ground. The propeller, engine, and seating accommodation should be covered over if covers can possibly be procured.

Keeping Up with the Art.—Finally let me urge that you read regularly some good paper on flying; I prefer *Aviation and Aeronautical Engineering*, whose publication offices are at 120 West 32d Street, New York City.

The changes and advances in aviation are taking place with marvelous rapidity and the way to keep up with all that is going on in the

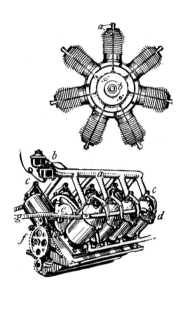

world of flight is to read what a corps of trained men have to say about it in the paper I have mentioned above.

Aviator Outfits

CAPTAIN GILL, *THE FLYER'S GUIDE*
(1916)

A pilot should be dressed properly to fly; not that he will fly the better, but that he may be more comfortable and that his landings may be made safer.

Aviators' suits are made to order by the A. G. Spalding Company and Abercrombie and Fitch, both of New York, and may be had in either khaki-colored or olive-drab army cloth. The breeches are like those used for riding, as shown on the opposite page.

Helmets with special padded tops and sides built on a heavy leather form with ear cones and felt lining, adjustable visor fronts, and extra protection at the back, as shown at B, are now worn by aviators. A leather hood, C, with wool fleece lining is worn underneath the helmet.

An Ilanasilk life preserver like that shown at D is worn by many aviators, so that if they should fall into the water their heads will be held above it. The safety device shown at E is used to strap the aviator to his seat. It consists of webbing straps, rings, buckles, and a releasing scheme that is bound to work when it is operated.

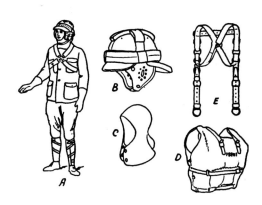

How to Remember Proper Names When Introduced

PROFESSOR LOISETTE, *ASSIMILATIVE MEMORY* (1893)

❧ ❧

AN INFALLIBLE method of remembering proper names is

(1) Get the name when introduced. If not quite sure, ask for it.

(2) Pronounce the name aloud whilst looking at the person. Do this several times, if possible. The object is to produce a concurrence or connection between the *sight-image of the person* and a *sound-image of his name*.

(3) To help the ear for sound, always pronounce everyone's name aloud whenever you meet him. This helps nature. These directions carried out never fail to make a pupil perfect in remembering proper names.

To remember *proper names* in the absence of the person, correlate the Person's Name to the name of some Peculiarity of the Person which you are sure to *think* of whenever you think of the Person. If you *memorize* the Correlation, you will recall the Name whenever you think of this Peculiarity (whatever struck you about him).

1. To what must we correlate a person's name?
2. What will be the result if we memorize the correlation?
3. To what do Mnemonists resort to remember proper names?

To remember a proper name, Mnemonists resort to "pairing." But this *alone* gives no starting point, no "Best Known" which you are certain to think of, and which will enable you to recall the name, *provided* you cement by a memorized Correlation the "Best

Known" to the name itself; in fact, a similarity of sound *alone* and *by itself* is likely to mislead you into reviving itself instead of the name. A celebrated Member of Parliament was to deliver an address at the Birkbeck Institution, some years ago. Having difficulty in remembering proper names, he thought he would *fix* the name of its founder in his memory by the Mnemonical device of finding a word that sounded like it; he said to himself, "It reminds me of 'Pinchbeck.'" He commenced as follows: "Before coming to the subject on which I am to speak this evening, I desire to pay a deserved tribute of praise to the founder of this great Institution, the celebrated *Mr. Pinchbeck.*" He could not remember the real name, Birkbeck, until it was told him. If he had mastered this System, his *new* memory-power would have enabled him to remember the true name *without any device*; or, if he was but a beginner at my System he could have remembered the name Birkbeck—which he was afraid he would forget—by correlating it to the word—"Founder," which he did remember, thus:—founder . . . lost way . . . hark-back . . . Birkbeck;

FOUNDER . . . foundered horse . . . chestnut horse . . . chestnut . . . bur . . . BIRKBECK. If he had memorized either of these Correlations, or one of his own, by repeating the intermediates forwards and backwards two or three times, and then recalled the two extremes, "Founder," "Birkbeck," several times, the moment he thought of Founder, he would instantly have recalled Birkbeck, one extreme recalling the other without the intermediates being recalled. When one has received only a third of the benefit of this System as a Memory-*trainer*, the mere *making* of a Correlation ensures remembering two extremes together without thinking of intermediates.

[Dr. Johnson, when introduced to a stranger, repeated his name several times aloud and sometimes *spelled* it. This produced a vivid first impression of the man's *name*; but it did not *connect* the name to the man who bore it. People who have adopted the Johnsonian Method sometimes remember the name but apply it to the wrong person, because they did not establish any relation between the name and the man to whom it belonged.]

HOW TO CAST A STATUE

GLASGOW MECHANICS MAGAZINE (1839)

❧ ❧

AFTER the artist has finished the model of the full size, he takes a mould of it in stucco; the separate pieces of this mould must be of such a size and form, as to part freely from the model.

The outside of this mould is now smoothed down, and that they may the more easily be put in their proper places again, each part has a number cut on the back of it; these are now oiled, and a cast is taken off the outside of them: this large outer case is made to part asunder in two pieces if the figure is not very large; the numbers cut in the back of each small piece will have made a corresponding mark on the inside of the large outer case; this enables the artist to place the parts in the outer case as he takes them from the model.

Let us suppose that the whole parts of the mould are placed in

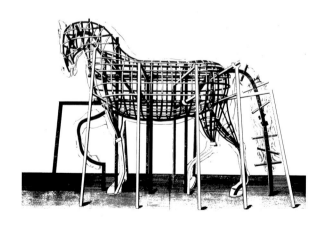

is also supported by having bars of iron laid into it bent to fit the form of the figure; the two halves are now joined and the whole set on end; the outer case is now taken off from the mould, and each of the smaller pieces removed from the wax. Corrections are then made by the artist on this wax figure.

Long pencils of wax are attached to all the parts of the figure from which the air will require to be taken—these are connected with the vents.

The founder now commences by coating over the whole with what he intends to be the inner surface of his mould, which is generally clay-water, and powdered-charcoal; loam is applied after the first coat is dry, and increased in thickness until enough has been applied; the whole is now built round with brick and strongly bound with screw-hoops, to prevent the mould bursting with the weight of the metal.

The whole is now dried with small fires placed round and below it; after a short time, these fires are increased to melt out the wax, which runs into vessels placed to receive it. When the wax is all out

the two outer cases as they ought to be, so that if the two were put together, they would be a mould fit to cast a solid figure: but this is not what is wanted, and a mould of stucco is only fitted for casting wax or stucco figures, as it will not stand hot metal; therefore, the artist lines the two half moulds with a sheet of wax of the thickness that he wants the metal to be, taking care that the wax is pressed properly into the mould that it may have a complete impression of it; the edges of each mould are smoothed that they may fit one another.

The whole is now filled with loam to form the core, having proper vents left to convey out the gas that may arise from the heated metal acting on the core. The core the fires are increased until the mould is heated to redness; it now requires to be treated the same as any other loam mould, that is, put into a pit and the sand rammed hard all round it to prevent the possibility of the metal either bursting, or otherwise making its escape from the mould; the core must also be well secured in its place, to prevent it from shifting or being buoyed up by the fluid metal.

After the metal has been run into the mould and cooled, the other materials of the mould are taken off, and the surface of the figure cleaned, the artist resumes his labor by cutting off the gates, vents, etc., making good any deficiencies by indenting, pining, and paring away any roughness until it is complete in all its parts.

This patching is required more or less in almost all works of this kind. In the pillar Vendome this patching is carried a great length. In the pedestal on which the statue of Bonaparte stands, many pieces have been indented, some of them as large as a page of this book, and this pedestal which forms the lantern is but a plain cylinder with a door in one side; the rest of the

parts of the pillar are too far from the eye for minute inspection, but all that you can get close to bears marks of it.

At the erection of the celebrated column in the Place Vendome, several faults were committed. This column was erected by order of Bonaparte, in commemoration of the victories of the French armies, and it was cast out of cannon taken from the Austrians and Russians in 1805.

The emblematic figures that form a band, making 22 revolutions round the shaft, were traced by Berzent, and were executed by 31

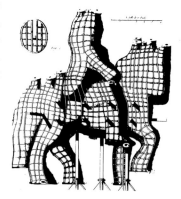

sculptors, one of whom was a female Mlle. Charpentier; the plates that cover the shaft are about 3 feet, by 3.8 inches high; there are 276 plates joined at the lower and upper edge by a spiral garter, on which was the inscription relating to each action; the plates representing this band is about 3 feet broad.

The whole weight of the different pieces of bronze composing it was 900,000 kilograms, or very nearly 2,000,000 pounds avoirdupois. The contract for the performance of the work was made with an iron founder, who undertook the whole, carving and all, for 1 franc a kilogram. M. Darcet, the celebrated chemist, tendered some good advice on the occasion, which was rejected, and the contractor had a foundery built, at a considerable expense. He employed a furnace for melting iron, and being ignorant of the fusion of bronze, he failed in his first attempts to cast the large pieces for the base of the column. At each operation he altered the proportion of the alloy, by oxidizing the tin, the lead, and the zinc, the oxides passing into scoria, or being partly carried off by the burning air. He did not perceive this, and delivered the different pieces of different qualities, but all of them contained a greater proportion of copper than the bronze of the guns. When the column was about two-thirds

finished, he found his supply of metal exhausted; and so sure had he been of having enough, that he had previously sold part of the 10 per cent, allowed him for waste, under the idea that it would be more than sufficient. Being obliged to complete the work with the quantity of metal delivered to him, he was placed in a disagreeable situation. Under these circumstances, he endeavored to cast the white metal obtained by reducing the scoria, and a quantity of old brass he purchased at a low price. The castings he obtained by mixing these materials were full of bladders and spotted with lead; they were at first of a dirty grey color, and afterwards became black. Such defective work could not pass, the labors of the undertaker were put a stop to; his foundery was sealed up, and the man ruined.

By dint of reclamations, he procured the appointment of a commission to examine his accounts. The commissioners wished to know the proportions of the different metals in the guns delivered to him; but this point had not been ascertained, and therefore the most important element for coming to a correct conclusion could not be obtained. The weight of each piece of casting delivered by him was known; and by taking morsels from them all, and melting them into one piece, an ingot was obtained representing the mean composition of the whole column. After ascertaining this, and knowing the general proportion of the alloys of which cannon are constructed, the commissioners agreed, in opinion, that the mean alloy of the column was equal to that delivered to the contractor. By analyzing the different pieces it was found that the large pieces of the pedestal contained only 6 per cent, of alloy, while the small pieces of the shaft and column contained 21. It was therefore evident, that the contractor, not understanding the nature of bronze, had refined his alloy in the first instance by repeated meltings; and having thus diminished very much the total weight, was obliged to have recourse to the means already described. At the commencement of his operations, he had delivered the pieces with too much copper, and at the end with too little. The pieces were, after all, so badly executed, that over 140,000 pounds of bronze were cut away by the sculptor, who was, moreover, paid 300,000 francs for his labor.

LEARNING TO SKATE

MONTAGUE S. MONIER-WILLIAMS, *COMBINED FIGURE SKATING* (1892)

❧ ❧

ANYONE wishing to learn to skate should read up on the subject before the cold weather sets in, and thus get some idea of what he is going to do. Then, having provided himself with the right kind of boots and skates, he should put them on indoors and walk about on a carpeted floor, taking care to avoid bare boards with their accompanying danger of nail-heads. By this means he will find out if his boots are comfortable and his skates properly mounted. The blades are not very liable to cut a carpet, but it is more prudent not to try them on one that is new or costly.

He should walk on his skates for a short time every day, and thus accustom his ankles to the varying strains thrown on them by the blades, as they are canted over to either side. At the same time he must stand erect and learn to walk on his heels, as this is the attitude he will have to assume on the ice.

The first time a man makes a start on the ice itself he should go alone, and must neither carry a stick nor lean on a chair; the chair may bring disaster, and the stick would be dangerous both to himself and friends. Indeed, artificial supports of any kind are more nominal than real, and tend to produce confidence in the prop rather than in the man's own self.

A good skater may render valuable assistance to a timid person, but must be careful not to allow a beginner to grow dependent on his aid, since it is self-confidence which has to be fostered in a skater, and any help given without true judgment discourages the growth of this all-important quality. Falls, moreover, are much more painful in imagination than in reality, and are of little consequence to a man who, finding that he is falling, will let himself go down without struggling; for the shock following an unsuccessful attempt to recover equilibrium is always much more severe than that which follows a simple tumble.

The Outside is the counterpart of the Inside edge; the body is canted outwards and the edge of the blade farthest from the unemployed leg bites the ice, the curve made by the skater tends to the right when he is on the right foot and to the left when on the left; but his attitudes on either edge are almost identical, the shoulder above the employed foot leads and the body moves sideways, but in this case the back is turned towards the center of the curve, while the face, as before, is turned the opposite way to the body at each stroke and looks forward in the direction of motion.

The skater should hold himself very erect and travel on his heel, and must force himself to lean strongly out to the right when on the right foot and to the left when on the left, and this he must do boldly, in spite of the feeling of insecurity caused, for the greater the confidence with which it is done, and the farther the body is canted over, the firmer will the skate hold the edge, and the less likelihood will there be of falling. In fact, the only real difficulty a man has to encounter, in learning the "Outside forward," is in making himself believe that he will not fall if he leans so far out to one side, and this fear is increased by the fact that, whenever he makes a half-hearted attempt to get on to the edge, his skate tends to slip sideways because it is not canted far enough over to bite the ice. A moderate amount of assistance, therefore, will often greatly help to teach a nervous person that he may safely trust himself to his skates, if he will only lean far enough over to feel the edge, but this assistance must be very slight, and should, if possible, be given by a good skater.

When a beginner has got away from the bank and is out on the ice, he should stay still awhile until he can stand erect and finds that his feet are not going to run away with him. He must, too, be especially careful to keep his center of gravity vertically above his skates, which means that he must stand upright and keep his feet beneath him, lest they slip out in front or

FIG. 1. OUTSIDE EDGE
FORWARDS (CORRECT).

OUTSIDE EDGE FORWARDS
(INCORRECT).

OUTSIDE EDGE BACKWARDS.

OUTSIDE FORWARD MOHAWK.

behind like the point of a stick on a polished floor.

He should after a time try to move forward by walking as on the carpet, and this he will find somewhat difficult at first, because one foot will retreat as the other is advancing. If, however, he starts with very short steps, and throws his weight gently forward on to each foot in turn as he puts it down, he will soon find himself to be traveling in the right direction. He must put his skate down pointing straight forward, and not try to correct or check its movement over the ice, but must let his body follow his feet and carefully keep the latter vertically below himself, so that the downward thrust of his weight may not tend to push them out from under him. If at any moment he feels he is going too fast he can put down both skates and glide on them until he comes to rest or runs into something.

He will soon be able to take longer and longer steps, and to throw his weight more forcibly and effectively forward at each one of them, while at the same time he will gradually lose the fear of being run away with. The more erect he stands, and the more he trusts him-

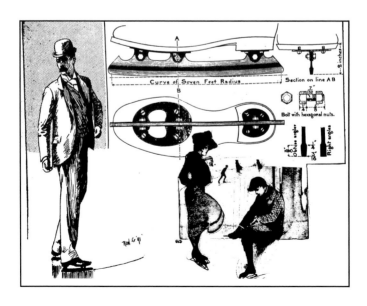

self to his skates, the sooner he will become their master and gain that confidence which is so absolutely necessary to a skater. Confidence and correct carriage are the beginning and end of skating.

As soon as a man can walk freely forwards on his skates, he must learn to push off from the ice with one foot, at the moment when he throws his weight forward, on to the other. He must make this push-off with the front part of his skate, which should be momentarily turned to an angle of about 45 degrees with the direction in which he is traveling. The front knee must be bent so that the hinder skate may touch the ice, and the whole stroke should be done boldly and with sufficient stoop to make it effective. But immediately the stroke has been taken, the front knee must again be straightened, the figure drawn up, and the unemployed leg allowed to hang close alongside its fellow.

The skater should strike off be-

ICEMEN

fore coming to rest, and while traveling at a fair speed, and must be especially careful to take every fresh stroke in the direction in which he is moving, at the moment; because any sudden change in direction necessitates a wasteful expenditure of energy, both in stopping the momentum of the body along, its old path, and in imparting to it a fresh momentum in the new direction. Whereas, if the direction be kept constant, no momentum is wasted, and only such as is lost, while traveling between the strokes, has to be made up at each push-off.

Pneumatic Railways & Rapid Transit in New York City

Thomas W. Knox, *Underground—or Life Below the Surface* (1874)

≈ ≈

For several years the people of New York City have been agitated on the subject of rapid transit from one end of Manhattan Island to the other. In one respect, New York is unlike any other city on the globe. Nearly all its business is conducted at one end of the island on which it stands, while nearly all the residences are at the other end. There is not a street car or an omnibus that is not packed to its fullest capacity in the morning, with people going downtown, and packed in a similar way about sunset, with people going uptown.

Travel at these times in the direction indicated is accompanied with many annoyances. On some of the lines of street railway, the passengers are stowed away very much like sardines in a can. Comfort is not at all considered. Very often passengers are wedged so closely that the movement of one affects nearly all the rest, and a person near the middle of the car finds it hard work to get out. Straps are suspended from horizontal bars running fore and aft the car, and

Section of the Broadway Underground Railway.

the standing passengers suspend themselves from these straps.

An ingenious individual has devised a plan whereby the space above the heads of the standing passengers may be utilized. He proposes some additional straps, on which a few passengers can be suspended horizontally, very much as dried fish in a museum are hung up against the wall. The position would be uncomfortable, but comfort is a secondary or tertiary consideration altogether.

The modern science of pocket-picking is very much in fashion in New York, and a goodly portion of the inhabitants seem to be engaged in an effort to make an honest living by robbing the rest. On a densely crowded car, one can frequently see gangs of pickpockets, varying from two to half a dozen persons, and unless he is very attentive, they will go through him without his knowing it. They are skillful operators, and the rules of the profession forbid the practice of the science until the artist is able to pick away a man's eye-winkers without his feeling it. I always look with pleasure on a man who boasts that no pickpocket can rob him. His confidence begets carelessness,

and the result is that he is generally robbed more than any other man.

The omnibuses are somewhat better in character than the street cars, though they do not afford accommodations for standing, especially if the passenger happens to be in the vicinity of six feet high. Many persons do stand in them, however, and revenge themselves for their discomfort by treading on the toes of the sitters at every lurch of the carriage. Intoxicated people do not ride in the omnibuses as much as in the street cars, partly for the reason that the majority of drunkards live on the railway rather than on the omnibus routes, and partly for the reason that it is not so easy to enter an omnibus as to enter a street car. The car has a conductor, whose duty it is to assist passengers on board and collect their fares, to kick off the disorderly ones, and keep everybody on good behavior. Between the pickpockets and passengers, the conductors generally occupy a neutral position, very much like the woman in the celebrated contest between her husband and a bear. The omnibus has no conductor, and as no one is responsible for the conduct of the passengers, they

PORTAL OF THE BROADWAY TUNNEL.

generally behave much better than on board a street car. If a man misbehaves himself in the former vehicle, his fellow-passengers eject him; but in the latter conveyance, the passengers do not wish to take upon themselves the conductor's duty, and as he is generally unwilling to perform it, it is not performed at all.

Time is an important consideration on these lines of travel. There are so many stoppages for landing and receiving passengers, so many blockades arising from vehicles in the street, and from other causes,

that the journey from end to end of Manhattan Island is not a rapid one. From the City Hall to Harlem, the ordinary time required is an hour and a half, and proportionally for other distances.

The question of rapid transit has been very much debated and several schemes have been proposed. Some inventors propose an underground railway, and some proposed a railway elevated sufficiently high to offer no obstacle to the passage of vehicles. A single track has been placed in the air on iron posts something like lamp posts, and carried from the Battery through Greenwich Street, and connecting streets and avenues, as far as Thirtieth Street. It is very doubtful if it ever gets any farther, or if anything more than a single track is built. The enterprise thus far has not met the expectations of its projects. It has swallowed up a great deal of money, and secured very little travel. It carries passengers at a fair speed, but it has had two or three accidents that have rendered the public distrustful of its accomplishments.

It possesses one advantage—that of enabling strangers to study the private life of the people on second story floors along its route; and for this reason I presume distinguished foreigners who come to New York are generally invited to make a journey over this railway. By no other means now known can so good a knowledge of domestic habits of New York be obtained. A gentleman who made a journey in one of the cars of this road soon after its opening, stated that he counted ninety-seven families at breakfast, of whom thirty-three were eating fish, twenty-seven were eating beefsteaks or mutton-chops, while the balance were sticking to bread and vegetables in various forms, or were breakfasting on nothing at all. He saw thirteen family quarrels in various stages of progress, and observed one lady discussing home affairs with a broom-handle.

Soon after this Elevated Railway was begun, some enterprising gentlemen undertook the construction of a railway under Broadway, on the pneumatic plan. They leased a cellar at the corner of Broadway and Warren Street, dug a tunnel under the sidewalk, and thence directly under Broadway for a distance of two hundred and fifty feet. It had been claimed that an underground railway could not be made beneath Broadway without interfering greatly with the traffic of that busy thoroughfare. The projectors of this line, known as the Beach Pneumatic Railway, contended that they could do their work without interference with travel, and they not only did it in that way, but they kept the entire public ignorant of their operations until they were ready to throw open the completed portion of their line for inspection. They were at work three or four months before any outsider obtained the least hint of what was going on, and for the last few months of their work the public dwelt almost entirely in conjectures. It leaked out that something was being done there, but what it was, nobody could exactly tell.

Finally, a certain day was fixed for the opening, and a great many persons were invited to be present. They found a comfortable station and waiting room under the side-be had at any moment with the engineer; and although the distance was short, the car, in moving along the track, attained considerable speed. They found powerful machinery, capable of forcing thousands of cubic feet of air per minute, and propelling the cars at a rapid rate. The machinery was moved by steam power, and the cars were propelled by the force of the air pressing against them.

PLACING THE LOADED SPHERES IN THE TUBE

walk of Warren Street. They found a passenger car on the track, and a well-lighted tunnel, through which they could walk, and listen to the rumbling of carriages overhead. The tunnel was as dry and comfortable as brickwork and whitewash could make it. Telegraph wires extended from end to end, so that communication could

Whether the tube was five yards in length or five miles, as long as it remained tight the car could be driven by the power of the stationary machinery.

Unfortunately for the rapid prosecution of the enterprise, the Pneumatic Railway was not, for the purpose of carrying passengers, a chartered institution; and up to the time of writing, it has never progressed farther than a single section, between Warren and Murray Streets. Its projectors have full faith in its ultimate success, and certainly the result of their enterprise, so far, has been satisfactory. They claim to be able to drill their tunnels for any distance, under any part of the city, without interfering with business; and they even propose to push their way under the East River, and thus extend their route to Brooklyn. They propose to have stopping places every half mile, where passengers can be taken up and left, and they promise to run their cars from one end of New York to the other inside of half an hour. They promise that there shall be comfortable weather at all seasons of the year, and are very certain that their route will never be blocked with snow. They assert that collisions are impossible, because their mode of propulsion is such that two cars cannot approach or go from each other on the same track at the same time. One of the great troubles of operating a line of railway by steam is the impossibility of making two trains pass each other on a single track. Many a railway engine-driver has attempted it, but on every occasion he has come to grief, and has generally brought some of his passengers to an un-

happy end. On an atmospheric railway the attempt to make such a meeting and passage is, from the nature of things, impossible; consequently accidents from this cause can never occur.

Another atmospheric railway proposed for New York is to be elevated in the air. An iron arch is to be thrown over the streets or avenues, sufficiently strong to sustain a great weight. On the top of this archway two large tubes are to be placed, each tube nine or ten feet in diameter, and having a railway track inside, where car-wheels can run. The pneumatic system is to be applied to the propulsion of these cars; very much as it is used to propel the cars on the underground line already described. It would possess most of the advantages of the underground system, and there is no good reason to predict the failure of a line constructed in this way.

Among the schemes that have been proposed for rapid travel and transportation of freight, there is one which purposes to make use of tubes, either under ground or on the surface, in which spheres or globes shall be placed, and propelled by means of a rapid current of air. The inventor claims that a sphere will move through a tube with very little friction, and can be driven with great rapidity. He would make a tube several feet in diameter, and have his spheres so arranged that they could be opened and filled with freight, then closed, properly fastened, placed in the tube, and started. I believe that he proposes to propel them one or two hundred miles an hour, at comparatively slight expense. For certain kinds of freight this mode of transportation and propulsion might be well enough, but there are things for which it would not answer. Imagine, for example, one of the spheres filled with fresh strawberries in Virginia for transportation to New York. The strawberries would be constantly roiled against each other, so that by the time they reached New York they would be in a condition of jelly.

As a passenger route this line would have great disadvantages. Imagine a man enclosed in a sphere, either doubled or laid out horizontally, to make a journey from New York to Washington. He would be standing alternately on his head and on his feet about

one hundred times a minute, and if he went through alive it would be a wonder, and he would be likely to be very much confused; especially if he were not packed tightly in his traveling-box, he would have a rough time of it. Every square inch of his body would be covered with bruises, and, besides, he would have a hard time to breathe, as the supply of air would be exceedingly limited.

I believe the inventor proposes that all parcels going by his route should be tightly packed; consequently, it would be necessary to wrap the passengers and secure them somewhat after the style of an Egyptian mummy, and stow them in their places by means of an hydraulic press. None of this mode of travel for me, if you please.

I have heard of a scheme of locomotion in which the inventor proposed to load his passengers into a large cannon, having a bore of three or four yards, and then shoot them to their destination. The journey could be made fast enough, but such a mode of travel is liable to accidents, both on starting and stopping. If one could get off and be well under way without being singed by the powder, he would run a great risk of being somewhat injured when reaching his stopping-place. "It was not the falling," said a hod-carrier one day, speaking of a tumble of twenty or thirty feet,—"it was not the falling that hurt me, darling, but the stopping so quick at the end."

Just as this book goes to press, it is announced that the Beach Pneumatic Railway has passed both branches of the New York legislature, and received the signature of the governor.

WALKING AND WALKERS

DONALD WALKER, *BRITISH MANLY EXERCISES* (1837)

❧ ❧

O<small>F ALL</small> exercises, walking is the most simple and easy. The weight of the body rests on one foot, while the other is advanced; it is then thrown upon the advanced foot, while the other is brought forward; and so on in succession.

In this mode of progression, the slowness and equal distribution of motion is such that many muscles are employed in a greater or less degree; each acts in unison with the rest; and the whole remains compact and united. Hence the time of its movements may be quicker or slower, without deranging the union of the parts, or the equilibrium of the whole.

It is owing to these circumstances that walking displays so much of the walker's character— that it is light and gay in women and children, steady and grave in men and elderly persons, irregular in the nervous and irritable, measured in the affected and formal, brisk in the sanguine, heavy in the phlegmatic, and proud or humble, bold or timid, etc. in strict correspondence with individual character.

The utility of walking exceeds that of all other modes of progression. While the able pedestrian is independent of stage-coaches and hired horses, he alone fully enjoys the scenes through which he passes, and is free to dispose of his time as he pleases.

To counterbalance these advantages, greater fatigue is doubtless attendant on walking; but this fatigue is really the result of previous inactivity; for daily exercise, gradually increased, by rendering walking more easy and agreeable, and inducing its more frequent practice, diminishes fatigue in such a degree that very great distances may be accomplished with pleasure, instead of painful exertion.

In relation to health, walking accelerates respiration and circulation, increases the temperature and cutaneous exhalation, and excites appetite and healthful nutrition; hence, as an anonymous writer observes, the true pedestrian, after a walk of twenty miles, comes in to breakfast with freshness on his countenance, healthy blood coursing in every vein, and vigor in every limb, while the indolent and inactive man, having painfully crept over a mile or two, returns to a dinner which his stomach cannot digest.

A firm, yet easy and graceful walk, however, is by no means common.

The Position and the Three Paces in Walking

In all walking, the position is nearly the same; but it may be performed in three different times—slow, moderate, or quick, which somewhat modify its action, and of which gymnasiarchs have described only the first.

Position in Walking

The head should be upright, easy, and capable of free motion, right, left, up, or down, without affecting the position of the body. The latter should be upright, having the breast projected and the stomach retracted, though not so as to injure either freedom of respiration or ease of attitude. The shoulders should be kept moderately and equally back and low; and the arms should hang unconstrainedly by the sides. The knees should be straight; the toes should form nearly half a right angle with the line of walk; and the weight of the body should rest principally on the balls of the feet.

SHORT STRIDE

The Slow Walk or March

This would perhaps, like the others, have escaped the description of gymnasiarchs, if military movements had not rendered such negligence impossible.

In the march, one foot—the left for instance—is advanced, with the knee straight and the toe inclined to the ground, which it touches before the heel; the right foot is then immediately raised, and similarly advanced, inclined and brought to the ground; and so on in succession. Care is taken to keep the sole, at the conclusion of the step, nearly parallel with the ground; to touch the ground first with the outer edge; and to rise from the inner edge of the toe. (Figure 1 and 2.)

The Moderate and Quick Pace

These will be best understood by a reference to the pace which we have just described; the principle difference between them being as to the part of the foot which first touches and internally last leaves the ground, and this being the circumstance in them which has been altogether overlooked.

We have seen that, in the march, the toe externally first touches and internally last leaves the ground; and so marked is this tendency, that in the stage step, which is meant to be especially dignified—as the posterior foot acquires an awkward flexure when the weight has been thrown on the anterior—in order to correct this, the former is, for an instant, extended, its toe even turned backwards and outwards, and its tip internally alone rested on the ground, previous to its being its being in turn advanced. Thus the toe's first touching and last leaving the ground is peculiarly marked in this grandest form of the march.

We shall find that the times of

the other two paces suffer successively less and less of this extended touching with the toe, and covering the ground with the foot.

The Moderate Pace

Here, it is no longer the toe, but the ball of the foot which first touches and last leaves the ground; its outer edge or the ball of the little toe first breaking the descent of the foot, and its inner edge or the ball of the great toe last projecting the weight. (Figures 3 and 4.)

Thus, in this step, less of the foot may be said actively to cover the ground; the footstep is in effect rendered shorter by the difference of the length of the toes; the pace is accelerated just in proportion; and this adoption of nearer and stronger points of support and action is essential to the increased quickness and exertion of the pace.

This pace has never been described either by dancing masters or drill sergeants; nothing quicker than the march has been attended to; people pass from that to the quick pace they know not how; and hence all the awkwardness and embarrassment of their walk when their pace becomes moderate, and

the misery they endure when this pace has to be performed by them unaccompanied, up the middle of a long and well-lighted room, where the eyes of a brilliant assembly are exclusively directed to them. Let those who have felt this but attend to what we have here said the motion of the arms and every other part depend on it.

The Quick Pace

Here, still nearer and stronger points of support and action are chosen. The outer edge of the heel first touches the ground, and the sole of the foot projects the weight. These are essential to the increased quickness of this pace. (Figures 5 and 6.)

An important remark has yet to be made as to all these paces. The toes are successively less turned out in each. In the grandest form of march, the toes, as we have seen, are, in the posterior foot, though but for a moment, even thrown backwards; in the moderate pace, they have an intermediate direction, forming nearly half a right angle with the line of walk; and in the quick pace, they are thrown more directly forward.

It is this direction of the toes, and still more the nearer and stronger points of support and action, namely the heel and sole of the foot, which are essential to the quick pace so universally practiced, but which, being ridiculously transferred to the moderate pace, make unfortunate people look so awkward, as we shall now explain.

The time of the moderate pace is as it were filled up by the more complicated process of the step— by the gradual and easy breaking of the descent of the foot on its outer edge or the ball of the little toe, by the deliberate positing of the foot, by its equally gradual and easy projection from its inner edge or the ball of the great toe. The time of the quick pace, if lengthened, has no such filling up: the man stumps at once down on his heel, and could rise instantly from his sole, but finds that, to fill up his time, he must pause an instant; he feels he should do something, and does not know what; his hands suffer the same momentary paralysis as his feet; he gradually becomes confused and embarrassed; deeply sensible of this, he at last exhibits it externally; a smile or a titter arises, though people do not well know at what; but, in short, the man has walked like a clown, because the mechanism of his step has not filled up its time, or answered its purpose.

I trust that the *mechanism and time of the three paces*, are here, for the first time, simply, clearly, and impressively described. I have not seen them even attempted elsewhere, which I think most discreditable to the people whose business it is to teach such things. It becomes indeed of real importance among certain classes of society and in certain situations; and I should be unworthy of my name if I neglected it.

Athletic sports, practiced as they are now, are often attacked on the utilitarian ground that the skill acquired in sprinting, or hurdling, or running many miles on a cinder path in spiked shoes, is such as can be of no practical advantage in ordinary life. Without discussing the general question at present, it can safely be said that there is one branch of sport to which, if properly practiced, the objection cannot possibly apply—we refer to walking. To learn to be a strong and fast walker must be of utility to almost everyone, and for walking matches there is therefore very much to be said. They lack popularity, doubtless partly because they are not exciting, and partly because it is still true, as was remarked by Charles Westhall the pedestrian the toe, in walking, upon the heel. In running, therefore, the body must be more or less thrown forward; in walking it must be almost, if not quite, erect. How then, they may well say, can it possibly hap-

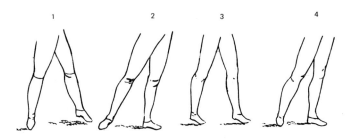

twenty-five years ago, that "walking is the most useful and at the same time the most abused of the athletic sports of old England." Now, as then, the public does not care for walking races, because when they go to see an athlete walk the probability is that they will see him shuffle, trot, or run.

To the uninitiated observer it may seem absurd that men who take part in walking races should, while they run, pass muster as walkers; because running and walking are perfectly different modes of progression. Running is a succession of leaps, walking a succession of steps; in running the weight of the body is thrown upon

pen that a man can run in a walking race without being discovered and disqualified? The question is a pertinent one and requires careful answering, but the real solution of the mystery is in our opinion this—that athletes, professional and amateur, have not arrived at a satisfactory definition, founded on a rational basis, of what fair walking is.

Westhall, writing in 1862 and speaking of professional pedestrians especially, says the unsatisfactory state of walking races arises "not so much from the fault of the pedestrians as from the inability or want of courage of the judge or referee to stop the man who, in his eagerness for frame or determination to gain money anyhow, may trespass upon fair walking and run." As Westhall was not only a good critic but a fine exponent of the art of fair walking, we can hardly do better than add some further extracts from his little manual. "The term 'fair toe and heel' was meant to infer that as the foot of the back leg left the ground and before the toes had been lifted, the heel of the foremost foot should be on the ground." (We might here observe that the more usual expression now is fair "heel and toe" walking, meaning that the walker places his heel to the ground before the toe.)

To these practical directions should be added another, which is implied in Westhall's description, but not explicitly stated, that at each stride the hip should be twisted round, the right leg being stretched out a little to the left, and the left leg in the next stride to the right, so that the walker's feet step almost in a direct straight line. By this twist round, each stride is lengthened and a corresponding increase of pace acquired.

The results of the loose practice of allowing "shifty" walkers to remain on the path are serious. The many naturally fair walkers who take up the pastime, when they find in races that more unscrupulous opponents "trot" past them with impunity, soon arrive at the conclusion that honesty is not the best policy, and upon the principle that *corruptio optimi pessima* become the worst offenders themselves.

Another result of the system is that novices learning to walk imitate their betters and so soon break into a run, leaning their body forward to trot as soon as they begin to tire. The result is what Westhall calls an "undignified" trot. The attitude is not only undignified, but is in most cases hideously ugly, which no fair running or fair walking is. In an ordinary walking handicap the public is thus treated to an exhibition in which more than half the competitors are in ridiculous and contorted attitudes. Naturally spectators are more inclined to laugh than to admire, and neither treat the affair as serious, nor take any interest in the result except upon the occasions when that rarest of specimens, the fast fair upright walker, is in the contest, when the interest immediately becomes genuine and unbounded.

In the early days of the athletic movement a seven-mile race was considered the proper test of a man's ability in this branch of sport, and a seven-mile race was the walking event included in the original championship program. At the present day the public find an hour's walking race rather a slow event to watch, and in most club meetings shorter races of three or two miles, and occasionally of one mile, are more usual.

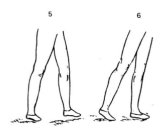

There are already plenty of temptations towards unfair walking and the production of a vicious style of progression, and with a shorter championship race the temptations will be increased. At present the one satisfactory thing about the championship walking event is that some of the shifty goers find it impossible to conceal the true secret of their mode of progression after the first few miles. The longer the distance is the more likelihood there is that a real walker will prove the winner, for besides the chance of detection, we believe it is really very hard to run on the heels for more than a mile or two.

Other Paces

It will be seen that the pressure of the right foot commences at the moment when that of the left begins to decrease; and that in all the tracings there is an alternation between the impacts of the two feet. The period of support of each foot is shown by a horizontal line which joins the minima of two successive curves. The impacts of the right and left feet are seen to have the same duration, showing that the weight of the body passes alternately from one foot to the other. It would not be the same in respect to a lame person; lameness corresponds essentially with the inequality of the impacts of the two feet.

In walking, the body does not leave the ground, the footsteps follow each other without any interval, and the weight of the body passes alternately from one foot to the other. The tracings, obtained by walking on a level surface, illustrate these points. There are exceptions, however, to this definition. For example, in mounting a staircase it will be observed that the step-curves encroach on each other, showing that each foot is still pressing on its support when the other has already planted itself on the next step. Besides this, it is at the time of this double pressure that the lower foot exerts its maximum force; it is at this moment, in fact, that the work is produced which raises the body to the whole height of a step. Nothing like this is observed in the descent of a staircase; the step-curves cease to encroach on each other, following one another very much as in ordinary walking on level ground.

A FINE FREE STRIDE

Forster Powell:
The Celebrated Pedestrian

LIVES OF THE GREAT & CELEBRATED CHARACTERS (1875)

❧ ❧

Mr. Powell was born at Horseforth, near Leeds, in 1734. He came to London and articled himself to an attorney in the Temple, 1762. After the expiration of his clerkship, he remained some time with his uncle, Mr. Powell of New Inn, and at his decease, he was successively in the employment of Mr. Stokes and Mr. Bingley, both of the same place.

Previous to his engagement with Stokes, he undertook, but not for a wager, in the year 1764, to go fifty miles on the Bath road in seven hours, which he accomplished within the time, having gone the first ten miles in one hour, although encumbered with a great coat and leather breeches.

It is asserted that he visited several parts of Switzerland and France, and gained much praise there, though his fame, as a pedestrian, was not yet publicly established; but in the year 1773, he traveled on foot, it being the first time, as it is imagined, for a wager, from London to York and back again, a distance of 402 miles, in five days and eighteen hours.

In 1778, he attempted to run two miles in ten minutes for a wager; he started from Lea Bridge, and lost it by only half a minute. In 1786, he undertook to walk 100 miles on the Bath road in 24 hours—50 miles out and 50 miles in—he completed this Journey three quarters of an hour within the time.

In 1787, he undertook to walk from Canterbury to London Bridge, and back again, in 24 hours, the distance being 12 miles more than his former journey; and he accomplished it to the great astonishment of thousands of anxious spectators.

The following year, 1788, he

engaged to go his favorite journey from London to York and back again, in six days, which he executed in five days and twenty hours. After this he did not undertake any journey till the year 1790, when he set off to walk from London to York and back again; he was allowed six days to do it, and accomplished it in five days and eighteen hours.

In 1792, he was determined to repeat his journey to York and back again, for the last time of his life, and convince the world that he could do it in a shorter time than ever, though now at the age of 58 years. Accordingly he set out, and performed the journey in five days, fifteen hours, and one quarter. On his return he was saluted with the loud huzzas of the astonished spectators.

In this same year he walked for a bet of 20 guineas, six miles in fifty-five minutes and a half, on the Clapham road. Shortly afterwards he went down to Brighton and engaged to walk one mile and run another in fifteen minutes—he walked the mile in nine minutes and twenty seconds, and ran the other mile in five minutes and twenty-three seconds, by which he was seventeen seconds within the time allotted him.

Having undertaken a journey to Canterbury, by unfortunately mistaking the road from Blackheath to London, which considerably increased it, he unavoidably lost his wager; yet he gained more by this accident than by all the journeys he accomplished; for his friends, feeling for the great disappointment he experienced, got up a subscription for his benefit.

Powell despised wealth; and notwithstanding his many opportunities of acquiring money, forty pounds was the largest sum he ever made by any of his feats.

In 1793, he was suddenly taken ill, and died April 15th, at his apartments in New Inn, in rather indigent circumstances; for notwithstanding his wonderful feats and the means he had of obtaining wealth, poverty was his constant companion. The Faculty attributed his sudden dissolution to his great exertions in his last journey to York. In the afternoon of the 22nd, his remains were brought, according to his own dying re-quest, to the burying-ground of St. Faith, St. Paul's churchyard. The funeral was characteristically a walking one, from New Inn, through Fleet Street, and up Ludgate-hill. The ceremony was conducted with much decency, and a very great concourse of people attended.

HOW TO TAKE A SHOWER BATH

W. BEACH, M.D., *THE AMERICAN PRACTICE OF MEDICINE* (1848)

❧ ❦

THE SHOWER bath is a species of cold bath, an invention by which water falls from a height through numerous holes or apertures, on the head and body. It may be conveniently made by boring numerous small holes through a tub or half barrel, which must be fastened a few feet above the head of the person. Another tub of a sufficient size to contain two pails of water, must be suspended over the other, and made to turn upon an axis. A rope or cord must be fastened to this, so that it can be inverted or turned downward at pleasure. The person taking the shower bath must place himself beneath, uncovered; and, having filled the tub with water, he will suddenly pull upon the cord, when almost instantaneously the contents of the upper tub or bath will fall into the lower one containing the holes, and the water will thus be conveyed in numerous and copious streams upon the head and body.

The apparatus should be enclosed, as well as the body, in a box or frame a few feet square, or large enough to enable the person to stand or turn round with convenience. A few boards or planks enclosed in a small frame is sufficient

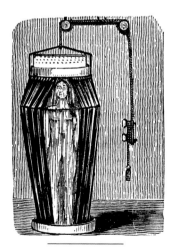

AN IMPROVED SHOWERBATH FOR THE CORNER OF YOUR ROOM.

for the purpose. Rub the body well with a dry towel after the bathing.

This bath may be used in all diseases of the head, epilepsy, nervous complaints, headache, melancholy, hypochondriasis, obstruction of the menses, and such complaints as arise therefrom, delirium, general debility, etc.

Dr. Sylvester Graham, who has become very celebrated on account of his lectures on temperance and diet, recommends, I am told, the shower bath for numerous complaints.

A writer in Zion's Herald, over the appropriate signature "Comfort," has the following interesting remarks on the shower bath, and his own experience in applying the same. We prefer it, whenever and wherever it can be used, to most other forms of cold bathing; and hope that its inconvenience will be obviated—at least in part—by the simple method which is here proposed.

"I had a shower bath made at the expense of ten dollars, and it makes a neat article of furniture in one corner of my chamber. On the top a box that holds about a pail of water swings on a pivot, and a string from it communicates inside; and underneath, to catch the water, is a snug-fitting drawer.

"Immediately on rising in the morning I shut myself in this enclosure, and receive the contents of the box at the top, let it drip off a moment, and then apply briskly a crash towel, and immediately a fine healthy glow is produced all over the body. The time occupied does not exceed five minutes: I have often done it conveniently in three or four minutes, particularly when the wind has been in a cold corner, and all cheerless out of doors; but in these melting times it is too great a luxury to be hurried through with.

"I hope all will be induced to try this plan who can possibly raise ten dollars to pay for the bath. I can assure them they will never put this article aside as useless, or sell it for less than cost. I certainly would not part with mine for ten times its cost, if another could not be procured."

The above figure represents an improved portable shower bath, which may be constructed at a small expense, and placed in a bedroom or other place. Both the bath and the water may be drawn to the desired height by means of the cord or rope running over the pulleys, and fastened to the ceiling. The person taking the shower bath is placed within, surrounded partially or wholly by the curtains, when he pulls a wire or cord which inverts the vessel overhead containing the water, and lets it fall in copious streams over the whole body. There is a receiver at the bottom in which the patient stands, and which prevents any escape of the water.

"The warm, tepid, cold, or shower bath," says Combe, "as a means of preserving health, ought to be in as common use as a change of apparel, for it is equally a measure of necessary cleanliness."

A bath on the above plan can be purchased for eight dollars.

Shower Bath Ring

A LADY USING A SHOWER-BATH RING
WITHOUT WETTING HER HAIR.

How to Be an Iceboat

Charles L. Norton, *Boy's Book of Sport* (1886)

❧ ❦

Very few skaters have not, now and then, to a moderate extent, made iceboats of themselves by standing up straight, with their backs to the wind, and allowing themselves to be blown along before it. Coats, held wide open, umbrellas, shawls, and the like, have been used to gain greater speed; but, after all was done, there remained the long pull back against the wind—no laughing matter, with the thermometer in the twenties, or lower, and a howling northwester sending the loose snow in stinging sheets along the ice. There was so much fun, however, in running down before the gale that boys have always made light of working to the windward. Why in the world it did not sooner occur to some ingenious lad that he could turn himself into an efficient iceboat, is one of those things that can not be explained; but certain it is that until quite recently the world at large did not know that Canadians were in the habit of rigging themselves with spars and canvas, sailing "close-hauled," "running free," having themselves "taken aback," "missing stays," being struck by squalls, and, in short, going through no end of fascinating maneuvers, with the aid of wind, and without danger of a ducking in case of an upset.

The name of the inventor of skate-sailing has not been announced, but his plan was the simple one of stretching an oblong sail on a light frame, and holding it by means of a spar reaching from end to end. With this, it is possible to do everything that an iceboat can be expected to do. But the crew works at a disadvantage: the steersman can see only one half as much as he ought to see, and of course stands in constant danger of colli-

sion. To lift or lower the sail, so as to see if the way is clear, is a somewhat awkward operation.

Another difficulty with this form of sail is that its spars must be somewhat heavy, in order to bear the strain of sufficient bracing, as there is a tendency on the part of the sail to twist and make a complete wreck of itself and crew. The latest improvement does away effectually with both these imperfections, and seems to provide a near-perfect device for skate-sailing.

In the first place, the sail is divided into foresail and mainsail, so that the crew has his whole course in plain sight between the two. Secondly, the main spar is made double, so that it affords two points of support for each of the "yards" or cross-pieces, and renders the whole affair so strong that

comparatively light spars may be used. In the diagram given, A G is the main spar, from eight to twelve feet long, according to the size and strength of the crew. It is made of bamboo, or some light native wood like spruce or pine. The pieces should not be less than an inch and a half in diameter in the middle. They may be tapered toward the ends, but one side of each should be left flat. Each piece, in short, is shaped like an archer's bow, much lengthened. The flat sides are laid together, and the ends at A and G are lashed firmly with strong twine. In or near each end, at A and G, is set a button to hold the clew—corner, that is—of the sail.

The most perfect spar yet devised is made of four pieces of bamboo, with brass fishing-rod

ferrules at the butts, fitting into one another at M. Brass tips hold the smaller ends of the bamboos together at A and G. The butts join at the middle of the spar, which can thus be taken to pieces and easily carried.

The sails are made from the heaviest cotton sheeting—unbleached is best. Tack the material smoothly on the floor, and mark out the sails, making ample allowance for heavy hems. Stitch stout tape all around where the edges are to be, and have the hem as strong as possible, especially at the corners, sewing through the tape and several thicknesses of the sheeting. If the sails are to keep their shape, the tape is indispensable. Stout laid cord (cotton or hemp), sewn around the edges and forming small loops at the clews,

makes a desirable finish, but is not absolutely necessary. Instead, small brass or galvanized rings may be sewn to the clews. These rings must be large enough to catch easily on the pins or knobs in the spar-ends.

The sails may range in size from three to five feet square, according to the size, strength, and weight of the skater. It is not difficult to arrange them for reefing, but they are so easily adjustable to the wind without reefing, that this is hardly necessary.

The cross-yards are quite light bamboo, five-eighths of an inch thick, at the smaller end, is probably heavy enough for the largest practicable sail. They must be made three or four inches longer than the diagonal of the sail. Near the ends of the yards are buttons similar to those on the spar. To the middle of each yard is firmly lashed a cleat, from three to five inches long, whose ends are shaped to as to receive and hold the two pieces of the main spar when they are sprung apart

Two opposite clews of the sail are now hooked over the buttons at the ends of the yard, the main spar is sprung apart until the cleat can be inserted and held at right angles between its pieces, as at J. The yard is pushed along until the clew of the sail can be hooked over the button at the spar-end. The other sail is then put in position similarly at the other end of the spar, and the two remaining clews, at C and E, are strained together with a strap or cord as tightly as the material will permit. The whole affair is exceedingly light, strong, and elastic, and will stand any reasonable strain.

Such is the rig. Now the question is how to manage it. This is a far less complicated matter than in the case of a sailboat, although the principle is the same. If you are caught by a squall, all you have to do is let go of everything, and your sails will fall flat on the ice and await your pleasure.

In running before the wind, all you have to do is to hold the spar across the course of the wind, steer with your feet, and go as fast as the wind does.

You can vary your course at will considerably to the right or left without altering the position of the sail.

When your course is nearly at right angles to that of the wind, or against it, you will naturally take the spar under one or the other arm, and point the foresail more or less in the direction from which the wind comes.

Let us call this second diagram a pond, with the wind blowing from top to bottom. In this diagram, the black spots represent the

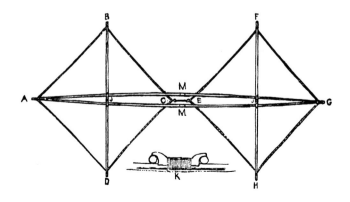

skater, the arrows the different directions sailed and the long line the spars and sails. In his first course down the middle of the pond, he grasps the spar by the middle, or holds it under his arms behind him. Squaring away with his back to the wind, as at A, he sails before it to the lower end of the pond, moving his feet only for the purpose of steering. In order to make the wind take him back to his starting point, he turns his sails at an acute angle to the course of the wind, as at B, C, D, and E, instead of across it as at A. If pointed nearly as at B or C, it will carry him directly across the pond. If as at D and E, it will carry him more or less up the pond, as indicated by the arrows. When he reaches the shore

Diagram for tacking.

on one tack—say that represented by E—he "goes about," that is changes the direction of his sails so that they point as at D. The wind will now carry him on a slant to the opposite shore, which he will reach at a point still nearer the head of the pond. Thus, by zigzagging from one side to the other, now on one tack and now on the other, he may work his way to windward.

Experiment alone can show each individual how best to trim his sails, whether to carry his spar under his windward or leeward arm, or before or behind him. Tastes differ in all these particulars. So, in going about changing, that is, from one tack to the other, each must adopt the method which he personally finds most convenient. One, perhaps, will pass the spar over his head; another will let the foresail fall off to leeward and bring up the mainsail on the other side, so that it will in turn become the foresail. In all these particulars, each must be a law unto himself; but in regard to avoiding collisions, it is plainly necessary to have a general understanding, and the rules of the Hudson River Ice-Boat Club, adapted to skate-sailing, are perhaps the best.

Rules for Skate-Sailing

I. Skate-sailers on the port tack must give way to those on the starboard tack.

II. When skate-sailers are moving side by side or nearly so, on the same tack, those to windward must give way to those to leeward when requested to do so, if there is an obstacle in the course of the leeward-most. But the leeward skate-sailer must go about or change his course at the same time as the windward skate-sailer, or as soon as he can without coming into collision. The new direction must be kept, at least until the obstacle has been cleared.

III. When skate-sailers are moving side by side, as in Rule II, and approaching a windward obstacle, the leeward-most must give way when requested to do so. But the windward-most must change his course at the same time as the leeward-most, or as soon as he can do so without coming into collision, and the new direction must be kept, at least until the obstacle has been cleared.

IV. When skate-sailers are running free, it rests with the rearmost ones to avoid collision.

V. Skate-sailers running free must always give way to those on either tack.

VI. Skate-sailers who violate any of the foregoing rules in the course of a race shall forfeit all claim to the victory.

VII. A touch, whether it is of a person or of a rig, constitutes a collision, either with another skate-sailer or with a mark or buoy, and he who is responsible for it, under the rules, forfeits all claim to the victory.

VIII. No means of locomotion other than that afforded by the wind is permissible during a race.

For the benefit of those who are not familiar with sea terms, it should be stated that "running free" means sailing before, or nearly before, the wind. "Close-hauled," or "on the wind," means sailing sharply across its course. When the skater's right side is presented to the wind, he is on the starboard tack; when his left side is presented to the wind, he is on the port tack.

The possibility of using the sail on an ordinary coasting-sled will naturally occur to every skater. This can be accomplished with the aid of a few additional fixtures. A regular iceboat has three runners, two in front and one in the rear. The latter is pivoted, so that it can be turned from side to side like the rudder of a boat, and used in like manner for steering. The first thing to be done with a sled is to provide it with sharp soes, which will not slip over the ice sidewise. A pair of skates,

or skate-blades, fastened one to each runner, near the bend, are as good as anything. The fitting of the after-runner is a more complicated affair, if fastened to the sled, and it is not worth while to give directions for it here. The simplest way is to let the after part of the sled rest on its own proper runners, and depend on the feet for steering, or use a stout stick shod with iron. A blade-shaped iron is best, as it presents an edge to the ice.

It is possible to kneel on the sled and hold the sail under the arm, but a mast about three feet high, stepped at the side of the sled, is better. If but one mast is carried, it must be arranged so that it can be readily shifted from one side to the other. The head of the mast is crotched to receive the upper spar; or a hook, large enough to hold it, and is inserted an inch or two below the mast-head. The lower spar rests against the mast, and is held there by the crew with one of his hands. A crew of two, on a long sled of the so-called "pig-sticker" variety, can do pretty work, one tending the sail and the other steering; but a crew of one will think that he needs at least two extra pairs of hands, until he gets the knack of the thing.

It is suggested that more sail can be carried by a single skater if his yard-arms are shod with light metal disks, so that they can be allowed to rest on the ice and act as runners. So far as known, this has not been actually tried. It looks promising, but will necessitate rather heavier yards.

FINGERSPELLING

SIGNS USED FOR LETTERS BY THE DEAF AND DUMB

❧ ❧

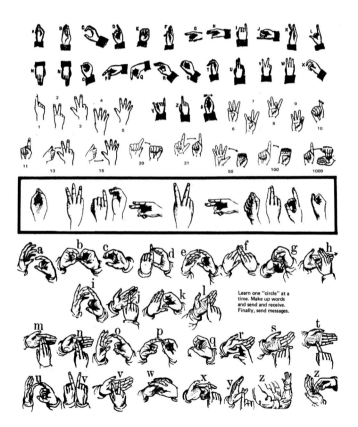

Learn one "circle" at a time. Make up words and send and receive. Finally, send messages.

HOW TO USE CHOPSTICKS

ST. NICHOLAS MAGAZINE (1890)

❧ ❦

WHILE A PAIR of chopsticks may seem to us to be the clumsiest of substitutes for the knife and fork, the Chinese and Japanese use them with such ease and skill that they are magic wands in their fingers.

"They cut their food with their daggers, and they eat with pitchforks!" cried the horrified Japanese who first saw Europeans eating in such a barbaric and revolting manner with the knife and fork.

Light-fingered, deft, and imitative as the Japanese and Chinese are, it takes them as long to learn the proper and graceful use of the knife and fork as it requires for us to master the evolutions and etiquette of the chopsticks.

It is a pretty sight, at the beginning of a Japanese or Chinese feast, to see the host help his guests to sweets, as then is displayed the best and most graceful play of the chopsticks. One can take a lesson, as the master of the feast daintily lifts cakes or confections and places them on the plate or paper before each guest. The Chinese

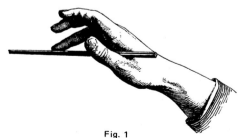

Fig. 1

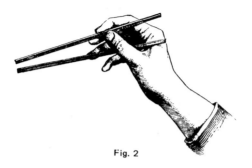

Fig. 2

chopsticks are longer than the Japanese, often metal-tipped and decorated, and are used again and again. Mandarins carry their own silver-tipped ivory chopsticks to a feast, wipe them clean, and carry them home again when it is over. In the common restaurants in Chinese cities, the chopsticks constitute a lottery for the patrons. All the sticks are kept together in a deep, round box, and certain ones are marked on the lower end with a Chinese character or number. The ones who select those chopsticks from the box are entitled to an extra dish or portion without charge. In the old city of Tien-Tsin, particularly, one is half deafened when he passes a restaurant by the rattling of the boxes of chopsticks and the shrill voices of the proprietors screeching the merits of their establishments at the top of their lungs, and appealing to the universal passion for gaming.

In Japan, where exquisite neatness and daintiness mark every part of household living, the same chopsticks are used only once. At a feast, or at an ordinary tea-house, a long paper envelope laid beside one's bowl contains a pair of twelve-inch sticks no thicker than lead pencils, whittled from clean white pine. To show that they have never been used the two sticks are whittled in one piece and split apart only half their length.

When the first course of the meal is brought in, one breaks apart his chopsticks, and placing one in the angle of the right thumb, braces it firmly against the tip of the third finger, as in Fig. 1. That chopstick is held rigid and immovable, receiving no motion except as the whole hand turns

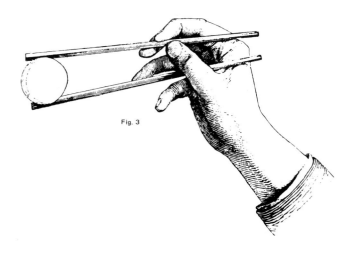

Fig. 3

upon the wrist. The other chop-stick is held by the thumb, first, and second fingers (Fig. 2), just as the pen is held in writing, and is the working member of the pair, moving freely, up and down or in any direction. A little practice will enable one to manage the chop-sticks with ease, and to hold them lightly, but so surely and firmly that they will not wobble nor lose their hold of anything. At first one will find his chopsticks making X's and crosses in the air, flying out of his fingers and performing strange and unexpected tricks in his help-less right hand. A traveler enjoys his meals at a Japanese tea-house, when he can pinch off a morsel of

fish with his chopsticks and dip it in the cup of soy, hold up a bit of fowl and nibble it, and do expert tricks with the convenient little sticks. Some small boys and girls whom I have known have become so infatuated with the chopsticks that they grumbled when they were made to use their knives and forks, and their parents would be in despair when these youngsters would suddenly be caught at the dinner-table "chopsticking" away at the meat, potatoes, or strawber-ries with the ease of natives.

The supreme proof of one's skill is to be able to lift an egg with chopsticks, or to transfer eggs from one basket to another. The smooth, rounding surface gives no good hold, and, after the perfect balance is found, too firm a hold will crush the egg or shoot it violently out from the sticks. I have often seen the proprietors of open-air tea-houses and wayside booths in a flutter of alarm when some rash foreigner began with his chopsticks to lift the eggs on their counters. But if the stranger performed the feat successfully, the Japanese would chuckle and caper with delight, and with deep bows gravely offer him a cake or a flower as a prize.

The Japanese rice is so glutinous that it is easily lifted up on the chopsticks in balls or lumps; but the loose, dry grains in a Chinaman's rice-bowl require a different treatment. He puts the edge of the bowl to his lips, and the two sticks are used as a shovel or fan, and sweep the rice into his mouth in a steady stream. Then the Chinaman presses the last grains in with the sticks, closes his lips, and sets down the bowl. All meat, fish, or vegetables are boned or cut into small pieces in the kitchen before they are cooked, and more than half of the dishes at an Oriental feast are soups or stews, rice accompanying every course as bread does with us.

The use of the chopsticks is not confined to the table alone. The Oriental cook will turn the cakes, or the chops, or anything in the frying-pan or on the gridiron with his chopsticks. The spoon or paddle is seldom used, and in a Japanese kitchen there is no pronged instrument equivalent to our fork. The cook stirs and beats with his chopsticks, and even spreads the icing on a cake with them, and rubs flour smooth in a cup of water. A Japanese cook will say "*naru-hodo*!" (wonderful), and a Chinese cook grunt something unintelligible if you show them a patent American egg-beater churning the white of an egg to froth with its ingenious arrangement of wheels, cranks, blades, and wires; but they both will put the egg-beater away on the pantry-shelf and go on beating eggs to a stiff froth with chopsticks—and do it so well and so quickly that one loses respect for the inventive genius of the age.

Two iron chopsticks fastened together with a chain (as our fugitive shovel and tongs of the fireplace might well be), always lie among the ashes of the bronze *hi-*

bachis of a Japanese house. With them, the masters or servants daintily lift the bits of charcoal and pile them in a compact pyramid, keeping the fire always to the center. The rag-pickers gather their stores and cull over street refuse with chopsticks two and three feet long. And at the public shops, where sweet potatoes are boiled and sold, a tubful of potatoes are covered with water, and by some sleight-of-hand stirring with these long chopsticks, are washed clean in the fewest minutes.

In raising silk-worms, the young worms that are too delicate to be touched with the fingers, are moved to fresh trays of mulberry leaves twice a day by means of chopsticks. The tiny, soft worms would be killed by rough handling with such clumsy things as fingers, but little Japanese girls lift them with their chopsticks so surely and so lightly as to do them no harm.

In the storehouse filled with the household goods which one of the Emperors of the eighth century bequeathed to a Nara temple, are several pairs of chopsticks, showing that the Japanese were feeding daintily at a time when the barons of England were using fingers and hunting-knives. The Chinese, of course, had the same dainty tools in use long before they invented gunpowder.

How to Have Good Posture

M. Lafayette Byrn, *Mystery of Medicine Explained* (1871)

❧ ❧

Proper & Improper Positions to Lie in Bed

CURVATURE of the spine may be caused by too many pillows upon which the head rests while in bed, as represented below. Young persons should lie as nearly level as possible, with the head but slightly raised if at all. As they advance in life, a more elevated position of the head may be desirable. Most people lie upon the right side; some lie upon the back, but this latter position is not favorable to those who are liable to night-mare. A frequent change of position is very desirable. If you awake during the night, change your position.

See how that round-shouldered youth is sitting with his shoulders against the back of the chair, and the lower portion of his spine several inches from it, giving his body the shape of a half-hoop. Parents should regard such a position in their children with apprehension as to the result, and should rectify it at once. The other young gent has learned a thing or two worth knowing, as you will see

by his manly, dignified position in his chair. He may be President yet—who knows?

An upright position, in either sitting or walking, favors a healthy action of all the various organs of the system, and besides it gives a graceful and dignified appearance to the human form. Children and adults are more or less inclined to lean forward with their heads upon their elbows, even when their seats are provided with backs; such a position oft-repeated must in time result unfavorably. There is a very "don't care" kind of look about one of these young ladies; if she lives long enough, she will care.

Learn to sit up, young man, and to imitate your opposite neighbor; for the unnatural position which you have assumed will never make you a good writer. An upright position, with the pen held loosely between the fingers, and determined purpose to imitate some definite copy as nearly as possible, is the only true road to success in the art of writing or good penmanship. This youngster on the left looks as if he was "bowing his back for a heavy burthen"— and so he is; if he don't quit it, he will have burthen enough.

How very distressing, and yet how common it is to see curved or

deformed spines. The habits of children, especially of girls, if not corrected in time, create a fearful frequency of this spinal defect. Na-

find a support for the back, and rest for the entire thigh-bones and feet, otherwise the bones of these, being soft and growing, are liable

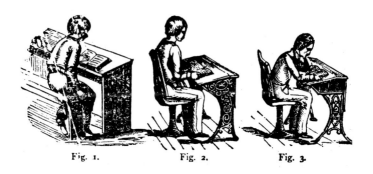

Fig. 1. Fig. 2. Fig. 3.

ture has given to all, both male and female, a sufficiency of bone and muscle to sustain them in the most graceful and healthy position, and when these are correctly and faithfully used, and their strength developed, they fulfill their intended purposes, and keep the form erect.

Old Style and New Style of Desks and Seats for Schools

Too many schools are furnished with seats at the same uniform height. If they are high enough for the larger scholars, they are too high for the smaller children. (See fig. 1.) In sitting, a child should

to become distorted, or out of shape. Fig. 2 represents a proper position, and fig. 3 an improper position, for sitting.

Examples

A form representing a full-chested woman. Such a person would naturally have a strong constitution, and could endure a great amount of labor, either mentally or physically. The European ladies are more generally of the above form than the American, because they take more interest in cultivating a full chest and fine form. In future let it be truthfully said that the

American ladies not only have "pretty faces" but healthy forms.

This is a facsimile in form of a great many women that are daily met with. Such persons are usually troubled with that sinking sensation, or "goneness" at the pit of the stomach, which is always produced by the pressure upon it in stooping, and might be prevented by

FORMS THAT CAN BE CULTIVATED

care in keeping back the shoulders, expanding the chest, and taking that kind of exercise so much needed, but so much neglected, called "House-work!"

This represents a man of stooping form, with small Lungs and

FORMS CONTRACTED
BY CARELESSNESS OR HABIT

Chest. Such a person would be almost sure to have some disease of the Lungs, Heart, or Stomach, and would naturally be Consumptive and short-lived, because the vital powers are small. Care should be taken to avoid contracting such a form. It is simply the result of carelessness and habit.

STOOPING FORM

HOW TO RIDE A RAILROAD TRAIN

DIONYSIUS LARDNER, *THE MUSEUM OF SCIENCE & ART* (1830)

✦ ✦

Rule I. Never attempt to get into or out of a railway carriage while it is moving, no matter how slowly.

SELF-PRESERVATION imperiously commands the observance of this rule, since forty in a hundred of the accidents which occur to passengers through their own imprudence, arise from this cause, and of these forty, twenty-seven are fatal.

It is a peculiarity of railway locomotion that the speed, when not very rapid, always appears to the unpracticed passenger much less than it is. A railway train moving at the rate of a fast stage-coach seems to go scarcely as fast as a person might walk. To this circumstance (which is explained by the extreme smoothness of the motion) is to be ascribed the great frequency of accidents arising from passengers attempting to descend from trains while still in motion.

Rule II. Never sit in any unusual place or posture.

Twenty-eight in every hundred of the accidents to travelers resulting from incaution, arise from this

cause, and of these twenty-eight, seventeen are fatal.

On some lines of railway, seats are provided on the roofs of the

carriages. These are to be avoided. Those who occupy them sometimes inadvertently stand up, and when the train passes under a bridge they are struck by the arch. Guards and brakesmen whose duty brings them to these positions, and who are disciplined to exercise caution, are nevertheless frequent sufferers.

Passengers should beware of leaning out of carriage windows, or of putting out their arm, or if a second-class carriage, as sometimes happens, has no door, they should take care not to put out their leg.

Rule III. It is an excellent general maxim in railway traveling to remain in your place without going out at all until you arrive at your destination. When this cannot be done, go out as seldom as possible.

Rule IV. Never get out at the wrong side of a railway carriage. All who are accustomed to railway traveling know that the English railways in general consist of two lines of rails, one commonly called the up line, and the other the down line. The rule of the road is the same as on common roads. The trains always keep the line of rails on the left of the engine-driver as he looks forward. The consequence of this is that trains moving in opposite directions are never on the same line, and between these there can never be a collision.

The doors of the carriages which are on your right as you look towards the engine open upon the space in the middle of the railway between the two lines of rails. The passenger should never attempt to leave the carriage by these doors; if he does, he is liable to be struck down or run over by trains passing on the adjacent line of rails. If he leaves the carriage by the left-hand door, he descends on the side of the railway out of danger.

On quitting a train under such circumstances, immediately retire to the distance of several feet from the edge of the line, so as to avoid being struck by the steps or other projecting parts of carriages passing.

Rule V. Never pass from one side of the railway to the other, except when it is indispensably necessary to do so, and then not without the utmost precaution.

Care should be taken before crossing the line to look both ways, to see that no train is approaching. The risk is not merely that of the train coming upon you before you can pass to the other side. You slip or trip, or otherwise accidentally fall, and a train may be upon you before you can raise yourself and get out of the way.

Precaution in this case is especially necessary at a point where the line is curved, and where you cannot command a view to any considerable distance. It is true that the noise of the train generally gives notice of its approach, but this cannot always be depended on, as the wind sometimes renders it inaudible.

Rule VI. Express-trains are attended with more danger than ordinary trains. Those who desire the greatest degree of security should use them only when great speed is indispensable.

The principal source of danger for express-trains arises not so much from their extreme speed as from their rate of progress being different from that of the general traffic of the line. If all trains without exception moved with exactly the same speed, no collision by one overtaking another could occur. The more they depart from this uniformity the more likely are collisions. Now the speed of express-trains is both exceptional and extreme. Inasmuch as it is exceptional, they are likely to overtake the slower and regular trains, if these be retarded even in the least degree by any accidental cause; and inasmuch as it is extreme, they are more difficult to be stopped in time to prevent a collision in such a contingency. If a collision occur, the effects are disastrous, in the direct ratio of the relative speed of the trains, one of which overtakes the other. The momentum of the shock, other things being the same, will be proportional to the excess of the speed of the faster over that of the slower train.

The probability of a collision will also be increased in the same ratio.

To work express-trains with safety, an additional line of rails should be laid down and appropriated to them.

Their number per day being necessarily small, and the duration of their trips short, the same line of rails might, without inconvenience or danger, serve for the traffic in both directions as on single lines of railway.

Rule VII. Special trains, excursion trains, and all other exceptional trains on railways are to be avoided, being more unsafe than the ordinary and regular trains.

There is always more or less danger of collision when any object on a railway is out of its customary place. The engine-drivers of the regular trains are always informed of the course of other regular trains, and, except in cases of accidental stoppage or delay, they know where they are liable to be encountered. Special trains are supplied on sudden and unforeseen occasions, and although their drivers are informed of the movement of the regular trains, and may therefore provide against collisions, this information is not reciprocal.

Excursion trains are exceptional but not unforeseen, and are not therefore as unsafe as special

trains. They are, nevertheless, to be avoided by those who scrupulously consult their safety. An examination of the statistics of accidents would conclusively prove the prudence of such a course.

Rule VIII.
If the train in
which you travel meet with an
accident, by which it is
stopped at a part of the line, or
at a time, where such stoppage
is not regular, it is more advisable
to quit the carriage than to
stay in it, but in quitting it
remember rules I, IV,
and V.

Rule IX. Beware of yielding
to the sudden impulse to spring
from the carriage to recover your
hat which has blown off, or a
parcel dropped.

It would appear that there is an impulse, which in some individuals is almost irresistible, to leap from a train to recover their hats when blown off or accidentally dropped. The reports of railway accidents supply numerous examples of this.

Rule X. When you start on
your journey, select, if you can, a
carriage at or as near as possible to
the centre of the train.

In case of collision, the first and the last carriages of a train are the most liable to damage. If the train

run into another, the foremost carriages suffer. If it be run into by a train overtaking it, the hindmost carriages suffer. Almost every case of collision afford an example illustrating this rule.

In case of the engine running off the rails, the carriages most likely to suffer are the foremost.

Rule XI. Do not attempt to hand an article into a train in motion.

On the London and Brighton railway, on the 15th of February, 1847, a passenger, while handing a basket to the guard of a passing train, had his coat caught by one of the carriages, and was dragged under the wheels and killed.

Rule XII. If you travel with your private carriage, do not sit in it on the railway. Take your place by preference in one of the regular railway carriages.

The regular railway carriages are safer in case of accident than a private carriage placed on a truck. They are stronger and heavier. They are less liable to be thrown off the rails, or to be crushed or overthrown in case of a collision. The cinders ejected from the smoke funnel of the engine are generally in a state of vivid ignition, and if they happen to fall on any combustible object, are liable to set fire to it. The railway carriages are constructed so as to be secured from such an accident, but private carriages are not so, and, moreover, from their greater elevation, when placed on a truck, are more exposed. Serious accidents have sometimes occurred from this cause.

The trucks which carry private carriages are also often placed at the end of the train, the least safe position. (See Rule X.)

Rule XIII. Beware of proceeding on a coach road across a railway at a level crossing. Never do so without the express sanction of the gatekeeper.

On the English railways, common roads are usually carried over or under the railway, which is crossed by or crosses them on bridges. This, however, is not invariable, and the greatest caution should be observed in passing such level crossings. A restive horse has fre-quently produced injurious or fatal accidents in such cases.

Rule XIV. When you can choose your time, travel by day rather than by night; and if not urgently pressed, do not travel in foggy weather.

Accidents from collision and from encountering impediments accidentally placed on the road happen more frequently at night and in foggy weather, than by day and in clear weather.

Persons on or near railways appear to be sometimes seized with a delirium or fascination which determines their will by an irresistible impulse to throw themselves under an approaching train. Cases of this kind occur so frequently, and under such circumstances, as cannot be adequately explained by predisposition to suicide.

WEATHER PROGNOSTICS

ERNEST BELL, *HANDBOOK OF ATHLETIC SPORT* (1890)

◅ ▻

Barometer

THE FOLLOWING rules may, in a certain degree, be relied on, as corresponding generally to the concomitant changes in the barometer and the weather:

1. Generally, the rising of the mercury indicates the approach of fair weather; the falling of it that of foul weather.

2. In hot weather the fall indicates thunder.

3. In the winter the rise indicates frost, and in frost the fall indicates thaw, and the rise snow.

4. If fair or foul weather immediately follows the rise or fall, little of it is to be expected.

5. If fair or foul weather continue for some days, while the mercury is falling or ris-ing, a continuance of the contrary weather will probably ensue.

6. An unsettled state of the mercury indicates changeable weather.

By these rules it will be seen that the words engraved on the plate are frequently calculated to mislead the observer. Thus, if the mercury be at much rain, and rise to changeable, fair weather is to be looked for. Again, if it be at set fair, and fall to changeable, foul weather may be expected.

Signs from the Sun and Moon, etc.

When the sun rises red and fiery, wind and rain are sure to follow.

If the rays of the sun, breaking through the clouds, are visible, then the air is filled with vapors and will soon produce rain.

*"But four nights old (for that's
   the surest sign,)
With sharpen'd horns, if glorious
   then she shine;
Next day, not only that, but all
   the moon,
Till her revolving race be wholly
   run,
Are void of tempests."*

—Dryden's *Virgil*.

If the new moon does not appear till the fourth day, it prognosticates a troubled air for the whole month.

When the moon on her fourth day appears pure and spotless, her horns unblunted, and neither flat nor quite erect, but betwixt both, it promises fair weather for the greatest part of the month.

When the wind veers about to various points of the compass, rain is sure to follow; but there is no prognostic of rain more infallible than a whistling or howling noise in the wind.

When the clouds are formed like fleeces, and very white at the edges, either hail, snow, or hasty showers of rain will soon follow.

There can be no surer sign of rain than when there are two different currents of clouds, especially when the undermost flies fast before the wind. When the dew lies plentifully upon the grass after a fair day, another fair day may be expected; but when there is no dew, and no wind stirring, it is a sign that the vapors go upwards, which will terminate in rain.

Against heavy rain, every cloud rises larger than the former; this remark foretells the approach of a thunder storm.

A dark thick sky, lasting for some time without either sun or rain, always becomes first fair, then foul.

*"The evening red, the morning grey,
Are sure signs of a fair day."*

Weather Wisdom

Weather wisdom is more necessary to the man who travels along the coast in a small vessel than to any one else. A large vessel is constructed to encounter any weather with safety, and she must take fair and foul as she finds it; but the safety of a small craft often depends entirely on an accurate forecast of the wind. When the skipper of the little yacht undertakes a voyage, say from Harwich to Rot-

tedam, he has to pick his weather. He waits in port till he gets a slant—that is, until he has satisfied himself that in all human probability no wind of dangerous strength will blow in the course of the next few days—then he weighs his anchor, hoists his sails, and speeds across the broad sea as fast as he is able, knowing that should a gale of wind spring up before he has made the opposite coast, he will be in considerable peril and not improbably be lost.

But the mariner who has made himself acquainted with the science of meteorology can make a coasting voyage, even in a tiny craft, from one end of Europe to the other, sailing from port to port in favorable weather, and dodging the storms that would infallibly destroy him, by foreseeing them and remaining in snug harbors until they have passed by.

In following the rules which we shall now lay down, the amateur will sometimes find that his forecast of storm will prove a false alarm and will keep him in port idle while he might have been at sea; but on the other hand—and

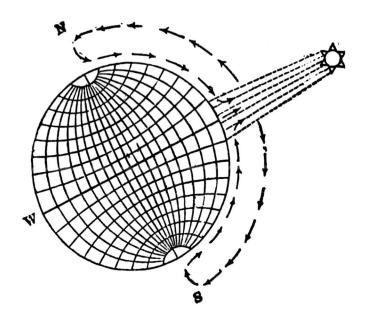

what is far more important—a forecast of fair weather is very rarely wrong; a really dangerous wind is scarcely ever known to spring up without having given a due warning of its approach.

If about to sail from any British port—for instance, across the Channel—in a small yacht, it is useful to remember that one can telegraph to the Meteorological Office, London, for a weather forecast for that particular voyage. The reply—the charge for which is one shilling—will be returned by telegraph without delay.

Such a forecast is more to be relied on than the opinion of all the weather-wise old sailors on the coast.

The weather can be foretold with considerable accuracy by observing the appearance of many natural phenomena, the clouds, the water, the sun and moon, and also by the movements of fish and fowl; but the changes of the barometer are far more to be depended on than the above as indications of coming weather.

Every small yacht should be provided with an aneroid barometer, which is more sensitive and indicates change more quickly than the mercurial barometer, also with a thermometer, and, if the yachtsman wishes to have a complete meteorological outfit, with a hygrometer or wet bulb thermometer. These three instruments will enable him to measure the weight, the temperature, and the degree of moistness of the atmosphere. The last of the instruments mentioned is not often found on a small yacht, and indeed the aneroid and thermometer suffice for ordinary purposes of weather-forecast.

It must be remembered, while foretelling the weather, that the barometer is affected—

Firstly, by the direction of the wind. The greatest rise being with the north-east wind, the lowest fall with the south-west wind.

Secondly, by moisture, an increase of which will cause a fall.

Thirdly, by the force of the wind. If a wind freshens, the moisture and direction of the wind remaining the same, the glass will fall.

These three causes do not often act in accord; one is generally affecting the glass in a way opposite to the other two. It is for this reason that an observation of the barometer alone will often mislead us. It must be read in con-

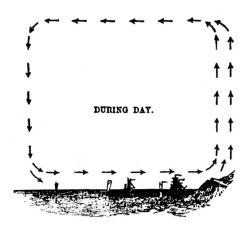

DURING DAY.

junction with the thermometer and also with the hygrometer, in order to determine the true cause of the rise or fall of the mercury.

Admiral Fitzroy's two well-known rules are—

The barometer rises for northerly wind (including from N.W. by the N. to E.), for dry or less wet weather, for less wind, or for more than one of these changes; except on a few occasions, when rain (or snow) comes from the N. with strong wind.

The barometer falls for south wind (including from S.E. by the S. to W.), for wet weather, for stronger wind, or for more than one of these changes; except on a few occasions, when moderate wind with rain (or snow) comes from the northward.

The following rules are selected from the official computation, which is very comprehensive and should be studied by every yachtsman. Admiral Fitzroy's book should be on every yacht's library shelf.

If the barometer has been at its ordinary height—about thirty inches at sea-level—and is steady or rising, while the thermometer falls, and dampness lessens, N.W., N., or N.E., or less wind may be expected.

If the barometer is falling, the thermometer rising, and the dampness increasing, wind and rain, or snow, may be expected from S.E., S., or S.W.

The most dangerous shifts of wind and the heaviest gales from N. happen after the mercury first rises from a very low point.

A rapid rise of the barometer indicates unsettled weather; a slow rise, or steadiness with dryness shows fair weather.

The sun's setting or rising behind a bank of clouds indicates rough weather.

A phosphorescent sea is a very certain sign of a continuance of fine weather.

The presence of vast quantities of jelly-fish presages fine weather.

Sea-birds fly far out to sea in fine weather; but if they fly inland bad weather may be expected.

When porpoises come into shallow water and ascend the river, stormy weather is near.

In conclusion, we will remind the yachtsman that the Meteorological Office issues a daily forecast of the weather for different portions of the British Isles. This forecast is now published in nearly all the leading morning papers, and should always be studied, if possible, before one starts across a broad sea in a little yacht; for it warns us of the "Yankee gale" that is on its way across the Atlantic, and whose approach has been announced by cable long before the barometer or appearance of the sky has given us any sign.

How to Eradicate the Disagreeable Skunk Odor from Clothing & Body

Andersch Brothers, *Hunters & Trappers Guide* (1906)

❧ ❦

To remove the disagreeable odor from the person, clothing, or skins is quite a conundrum. Following are the best methods.

First—Hang the clothing up on a line and give garments necessary airing.

Second—Rinse clothing so affected in a bath of moist hardwood sawdust. If the sawdust is perfumed, so much the better.

Third—Rinse clothing affected by the disagreeable odor of the skunk stink and civet cat in gasoline or benzine. Immerse them numerous times, then rinse and hang out on line to dry. While doing this never smoke or permit any fire in the immediate vicinity. If you can obtain naphtha, so much the better. Obtain sufficient to cover clothing and rinse two or three times. Hang on the line and the naphtha will evaporate in very short order, and with it the odor.

Fourth—Wrap affected garments up in hemlock bark or place in moist crumbs of bark. Within twenty-four hours the clothing will be ready to put on.

Fifth—Hold affected garments over fire of red cedar boughs and when they are saturated with the smoke and odor coming from the burning boughs, hang up on a line to air out. If cedar is unobtainable, use hemlock boughs or burn large quantities of pine needles.

Sixth—To eradicate this disagreeable smell from the body, especially the hands, one can use naphtha, gasoline, or kerosene and finish by eradicating odor of these oils, as well as the original odor, by washing the hands or other portions of the body with tar soap. Strong soapsuds from tar soap will remove the skunk odor quite frequently alone.

At the tannery, skins are packed

in moist hemlock sawdust, washed in soapsuds, or at times the odor is counteracted by the use of perfumes. If skins are not badly saturated, no attention is paid, as in the process of cleaning in the large revolving drums which contain fine, dry, hard-wood sawdust, the skins come out free from odor. These drums make about twenty revolutions per minute and the furs fall on pegs; at every revolution they are submerged in the sawdust, which not only tends to eradicate all odor, but also cleanses the fur thoroughly. After this process the furs are freed from sawdust by shaking.

Never use chloride of lime as that destroys the clothing. Neither is it a good policy to bury the clothing in the ground, as that tends to keep the nuisance within them, unless the pieces are spread out and then covered with fine, damp earth.

The skunk, although armed with claws and teeth strong

enough to capture his prey, is slow on foot, apparently timid, and would be unable to escape from many of his enemies if he were not possessed of a power by which he often causes the most ferocious to make a rapid retreat, run the nose into the earth, or roll and tumble on the ground as if in convulsions; and not infrequently even the bravest of our boasting race is by this little animal compelled suddenly to break off his train of thought, hold his nose and rue as if a lion were at his heels.

The skunk in general appearance is always neat and clean, and in walking seemingly takes special pride, as when promenading, its tail is erect and its back peculiarly curved. Very few animals are as harmless as this creature and were it not for the peculiar odor which it distributes when in danger, it would be more hunted and probably eradicated in sections. Its principal weapon, as heretofore noted, is a peculiar secretion and fluid possessing a very disagreeable odor. This fluid is of a pale yellow color and is discharged by the animal when in danger, in thinnish streams and with such accuracy and aim as to strike any object within 6 to 12 feet. The fluid is secreted in two anal glands from which by the contraction of the sub-caudal muscles and by uplifting of the tail it is discharged in the form as above stated. Trappers who are familiar with this secretion state that the discharge of this perfume looks like a puff of steam or white smoke. Dogs and other animals are adverse to attacking a skunk and only inexperienced or so-called "tenderfeet" will view this animal from the rear unless at a great distance.

The animal passes the winter season in a state of incomplete hibernation, and at regular intervals he will arise, come out of his abode and expose his body to the sun, and judging from the effluvium, empty its distended pouches, but the stench thus caused soon ceases, which is not the case when it is spurted under irritation or in self-defense. Dr. Coues states "that the animal uses this secretion in the relation of its perpetuation of the species, though overshadowed by its exaggeration into a powerfully effective means of preservation of the individual, is evidently the same as in other species of *Mustelidae*, each one of which has its own emanation to bring the sexes together, not only by simply indicating their whereabouts, but by serving as a positive attraction. In the case of the skunk, it would seem that the strong scent has actually tended to result in a more gregarious mode of life than is usual in this family of mammals; and it is certain, at any rate, that the occupancy by one animal of a permanent winter abode serves to attract others to the same retreat. Burrows are sometimes found to contain as many as a dozen individuals, not members of one family, but various adult animals drawn together. One other effect of the possession of such unique powers is seen not so much in mode of life as in the actual disposition of the creature. Its heedless familiarity, its temerity in pushing into places which other animals instinctively avoid as dangerous, and its indisposition to seek safety by hasty retreat, are evident results of its confidence in the extraordinary means of defense with which it is provided. In speculating upon the development of this anal armature to a degree which renders it subservient to purposes for which the glands of other *Mustelidae*, though of similar character, are manifestly inadequate, and it may not be amiss to recall how defenseless the skunk would otherwise be in comparison with its allies. A tardy, terrestrial animal of no great strength of spirit, lacking the sagacity and prowess of the wolverine, the scansorial ability of the marten, the agility, small size, and tenuity of body of the weasel, the swimming and diving powers of the otter, and even much of the eminent fossorial capacity of its nearest relations, the badger—lacking all these qualities, which in their several exhibitions conduce to the safety of the respective species, it is evident that additional means of self-protection were required; while the abundance of the animal in most parts of the country, and its audacity in the face of danger, show that its confidence in the singular means of defense it possesses is not misplaced.

THE BEDROOM CHAIR AS GYMNASIUM

W. R. LATSON, M. D., *COMMON DISORDERS* (1904)

❧ ❦

ALTHOUGH there is no doubt in my personal opinion that the highest possible degree of physical perfection may be attained by the practice of "free" gymnastics—that is, of gymnastics without apparatus—yet it is undoubtedly true that the practice of "free" exercise is to many people less interesting than movements made in connection with some apparatus or instrument.

The disadvantages of apparatus gymnastics are often due not as much to their use as to their abuse. For instance, the main injuries due to apparatus work are local development (that is, undue development of one part at the expense of the general physical welfare) and overstrain. These should be guarded against, and both can be prevented by using proper apparatus, by moderation, and by corrective exercise. Apparatus should be simple and convenient and should be of such a nature that in using it, the muscles of the entire body can be exercised.

As an apparatus for gymnastics, the bedroom chair meets these requirements quite fully. It is simple, it is convenient, and it can be used in movements which bring into action practically every important muscle in the body.

The series of exercises described below have been carefully devised with a view, first, to the formation of proper habits of car-

riage; second, to increase the activity of the internal organs; third, to the development of the general muscular system, and, fourth, to the encouragement of grace and bodily poise.

These exercises should be practiced exactly as described and should always be followed by relaxing exercises, as otherwise they would tend to stiffen the muscles and interfere with the grace and freedom of motion. The time devoted to them will vary with the strength of the student. Another point is the weight of the chair used. For a weak person, the lightest obtainable chair is quite heavy enough. The robust may execute the movements with a heavier chair.

Care should be taken that there is sufficient room to swing the chair without doing damage.

Exercise No. 1.

Place the chair in front of you and grasp the seat with both hands, arms straight. Now, take full breath, and, still keeping the hands in position, step backward until the feet are so far distant from chair as to throw the weight of the body largely upon the arms. Then,

still holding the breath, straightening the arms, raise the body to its original position. Notice that the farther from the chair you place the feet, the more is thrown upon the hands and the more severe becomes the exercise. (See Fig. 1.)

This movement is of value in broadening and deepening the chest, in replacing round shoulders and protruding collar bones, and

Exercise No. 2.

Stand in front of chair as in previous exercise. Now take breath, reach forward and grasp the back of the chair (as shown in Fig. 2). Straighten the body, holding the chair, as shown in the figure. Then, without bending the body and still holding the lungs full of air, slowly lift the chair upward by bending the arms, until it is on a

in developing the muscles of the chest, back, shoulders, and arm. It is particularly useful in increasing the size and power of the triceps, which is the largest, handsomest, and perhaps the most useful muscle in the arm. The triceps lies at the back of the arm and is used in all pushing and thrusting actions.

level with the head. Then lower to the floor, after which the lungs may be deflated, allowing the breath to escape in a gentle sigh. This exercise especially develops the front of the upper arm, the biceps, the muscles of the forearm, also certain important muscles of the back and shoulders.

Exercise No. 3.

Stand in front of the chair and grasp seat, as in Exercise No. 1. Then, holding head, chest, arms, and shoulders rigid, gradually straighten the back, lifting the chair up to a level with the head. (See Fig. 3.)

This movement calls for acti-vity of the powerful and important muscles of the back. In all lifting, bending, or similar exertion, in walking, running, or stair climbing, these muscles of the back have an important function in sustaining the weight of the superincumbent body.

Exercise No. 4.

Stand exactly as shown in Figure 3, body motionless, lungs full. Now, holding the upper part of the body motionless, swing the body as on a pivot around to the right as far as possible, without moving feet. Then turn to the left, twisting the body from the legs upward, still holding the chair extended.

This movement is designed to call into action all the muscles of the body, bearing especially upon the muscles of the waist. The muscles of the lumbar region ("the small of the back") and the abdominal are by far the most important muscles in the body. Whatever work is being done by the limbs, it must be supported by the waist muscles. A man who is weak here is weak all over. A woman, who by inactivity or corseting has allowed these muscles to become weak, will suffer from a dozen ailments directly traceable thereto. The last two exercises have been especially devised to bring these muscles into activity, and their practice cannot fail to strengthen this most important region.

Exercise No. 5.

Stand with chair back toward you. Place feet well apart. Take deep breath and hold same during the exercise. Grasp chair by the back, raise it in front and swing it slowly around to right, throwing weight of the body on the right leg. Then swing it around in front and to the left in a wide circle. And so from one side to the other two or three times. Then lower the chair to the floor and exhale breath. (See Fig. 4.)

Exercise No. 6.

Stand easily, feet well apart, take breath and hold during the exercise. Grasp chair by the back, as in Exercise No. 5, but higher up. (See Fig. 5.) Now bend arms until the forearms are on a level with the elbows. Then swing the chair gently from side to side, keeping the arms in about the same position and allowing the chair to swing from them with a pendulum-like motion.

This exercise develops the entire arm, shoulder, and chest and calls for general activity of the muscles of the back, abdomen, and legs.

Of course, these chair exercises are of greatest possible value in de-

veloping hands, wrists, and forearms. They are also useful in developing general muscular control and coordination.

Useful, however, as are these chair exercises, they will be certain to interfere with perfect grace and freedom of motion unless they are practiced in connection with certain corrective exercises. The best corrective movements for this purpose are the following:

Exercise. No. 7.

Stand easily, one foot slightly advanced. Now inhale breath, at the same time raising the arms, chest, and face until all are stretched

firmly upward. (See Fig. 6.) Then, without pause or holding the breath, allow arms, head, and body to fall limply forward toward the floor, at the same time exhaling the breath in a gentle sigh. (See Fig. 7.)

Exercise No. 8.

Stand easily, feet well apart, swing arms and body gently from side to side, imitating the motions of a man scattering grain. Do this as gently as possible, allowing the whole body and the head to swing in harmony with the arms.

Exercises with a chair should always be followed by the practice of Exercises Nos. 7 and 8, for the purpose of preventing the rigidity which is always certain to follow any severe muscular exertion, unless corrected by relaxing movements.

As a whole, the practice of this simple system of chair exercises will bring about results that will surprise many; while many of those who practice them for the first time will discover a new interest and utility in this very prosaic article of furniture.

THE ELEPHANT AT WORK

JOHN R. CORYELL, *SCRIBNER'S*, (1887)

❧ ❧

LAZY AND clumsy-looking as the elephant appears in our menageries, where it is merely an object of curiosity, in Asia it is as useful an animal as the horse, and is, indeed, employed in a greater variety of ways. There are few, if any, tasks which a horse can be trusted to perform without careful and constant guidance; whereas the elephant is frequently given as much independence of action as a man would have for the same work. This is notably the case in the lumber-yards of Rangoon and Maulmein, where the entire operation of moving and piling the heavy timber is performed by male elephants without any special supervision by the keepers.

The logs to be moved are teakwood, which is very heavy. They are cut into lengths of twenty feet, with a diameter, or perhaps a square, of about a foot. An elephant will go to a log, kneel down, thrust his tusks under the middle of it, curl his trunk over it, test it to see that it is evenly balanced, and then rise with it and easily carry it to the pile which is being made. Placing the log carefully on the pile in its proper place, the sagacious animal will step back a few paces and measure with his eye to determine whether or not the log needs pushing one way or another. It will then make any necessary alteration of position. In this way, without a word of command from its mahout, or driver, it will go on with its work.

To do any special task, it must, of course, be directed by the mahout; but it is marvelous to see how readily this great creature comprehends its instructions, and how ingeniously it makes use of its strength. If a log too heavy to be carried is to be moved a short distance, the elephant will bend low,

place his great head against the end of the log and then with a sudden exertion of strength and weight throw his body forward and fairly push the log along; or, to move the log any great distance, he will encircle it with a chain—using his trunk for that purpose—and drag his load behind him.

As a rule, however, the work of dragging is done by the female elephants, since, having no tusks, they can not carry logs as the male elephants do. A man could hardly display more judgment in the adjustment of the rope or chain around a log, nor could a man with his two hands tie and untie knots more skillfully than do they with their trunks.

In some parts of India the elephant is used to drag the plow, and, though it seems from its great strength and size unfit for such work, yet so docile and intelligent is it, that it performs the task as satisfactorily as the horse.

It is owing to its combined docility, intelligence, strength, and suppleness that it is enabled to perform the extraordinary tasks imposed upon it—tasks which range between two such extremes as child's nurse and public executioner. It is not often, perhaps, that the elephant acts in the latter capacity, but in the former it frequently does—ably, too, for the monstrous beast seems to have a natural affection for babies, whether human or otherwise.

In India, where the elephant is treated by his mahout almost as one of the family, the grateful animal makes a return for the kindness shown it by voluntarily taking care of the baby. It will patiently permit itself to be mauled by its little charge, and will show great solicitude when the child cries. Sometimes the elephant will become so attached to its baby friend as to insist upon its constant presence. Such a case is known where the elephant went so far as to refuse to eat except in the presence of its little friend. Its attachment was so genuine that the child's parents would not hesitate to leave the baby in the elephant's care, knowing it could have no more faithful nurse. And the kindly monster never belied the trust reposed in it. If the flies came about the baby, it would drive them away. If the baby cried, the giant nurse would rock the cradle until the little thing slept.

Nor are only the female elephants so affectionate with the helpless little ones; the male animals are equally kind. Perhaps this is because the fathers as well as the

mothers among the wild elephants have the care of the elephant babies. Mr. G. F. Holder contributes several interesting incidents in this connection. In a paper on the subject he says: "How the young elephants, in the large herds, escape from being crushed, is something of a mystery, as they are almost continually in motion; but when a herd is alarmed, the young almost immediately disappear. A close observer would see that each baby was trotting along directly beneath its mother, sometimes between her fore legs, and in various positions; and so careful are the great mothers and fathers, that even while a herd is charging, the little ones are never crushed or stepped upon.

"On the march, when a little elephant is born in a herd, they stop a day or two to allow it time to exercise its little limbs and gain strength, and then they press on, the mothers and babies in front, the old tuskers following in the rear, but ready to rush forward at the first alarm. When rocky or hilly places are reached, the little ones are helped up by the mothers, who push them from behind and in various ways; but when a river has to be forded or swum a comical sight ensues.

"The stream may be very rapid and rough, as the Indian rivers often are after a rain, and at such a place the babies would hardly be able to keep up with the rest; so the mothers and fathers help them. At first all plunge boldly in—both young and old—and when the old elephants reach deep water, where they have to swim, the young scramble upon their

backs and sit astride, sometimes two being seen in this position. But the very young elephants often require a little more care and attention, so they are held either upon the tusks of the father or grasped in the trunk of the mother, and held over or just at the surface of the water. Such a sight is a curious one, to say the least—the great elephants almost hidden beneath the water, here and there a young one seemingly walking on the water, resting upon a submerged back, or held aloft while the dark waters roar below."

How to Shake Hands

Accompanying the salutation of hand-shaking, it is common, according to the customs of English-speaking people, to inquire concerning the health, the news, etc.

Offer the whole hand. It is an insult, and indicates snobbery, to present two fingers (Fig. 1) when shaking hands. It is also insulting to return a warm, cordial greeting with a lifeless hand (Fig. 2), and evident indifference of manner, when hand-shaking. Present a cordial grasp (Fig. 3) and clasp the hand firmly, shaking it warmly for a period of two or three seconds, and then relinquish the grasp entirely. It is rude to grasp the hand very tightly or to shake it over-vigorously. To hold it a long time is often very embarrassing, and is a breach of etiquette. It is always the lady's privilege to extend the hand first. In her own house a lady should give her hand to every guest.

FIG. 1. THE SNOB THAT STICKS OUT TWO FINGERS
WHEN SHAKING HANDS

If both parties wear gloves, it is not necessary that each remove them in shaking hands; if one, however, has ungloved hands, it is courtesy for the other to remove the glove, unless in so doing it would cause an awkward pause; in which case apologize for not removing it, by saying, "Excuse my glove." The words and forms will always very much depend upon circumstances, of which the individuals can themselves best judge. Kid and other thin gloves are not expected to be removed in handshaking; hence, apology is only necessary for the non-removal of the thick, heavy glove.

As a rule in all salutations, it is well not to exhibit too much haste.

FIG. 2. THE COLD-BLOODED, LANGUID PERSON, THAT EXHIBITS ONLY INDIFFERENCE AS YOU SHAKE THE HAND.

FIG. 3. THE GENEROUS, FRANK, WHOLE-SOULED INDIVIDUAL THAT GREETS YOU WITH A WARM, HEARTY GRASP.

The cool, deliberate person is much the most likely to avoid mistakes. The nervous, quick-motioned, impulsive individual will need to make deliberation a matter of study; else, when acting on the spur of the moment, with possibly slight embarrassment, ludicrous errors are liable to be made. In shaking hands, offer the right hand, unless the same be engaged; in which case, apologize, by saying "Excuse my left hand." It is the right hand that carries the sword in time of war, and its extension is emblematic of friendliness in time of peace.